# He's Worth *the* Wait

**REDEMPTION**
PRESS

# He's Worth *the* Wait

## The Christian Gal's Guide to
## DATING AND WAITING

---

# JOLENE SAUNDERS

Published by Redemption Press, PO Box 427, Enumclaw, WA 98022.

Toll-Free (844) 2REDEEM (273-3336)

Redemption Press is honored to present this title in partnership with the author. The views expressed or implied in this work are those of the author. Redemption Press provides our imprint seal representing design excellence, creative content, and high-quality production.

ISBN: 978-1-64645-104-3 (Paperback)
978-1-64645-105-0 (ePub)
978-1-64645-106-7 (Mobi)

Library of Congress Catalog Card Number: 2020909885

# Contents

# Introduction

I've dated the liar, the gambler, the drug addict, the alcoholic, the wealthy, the homeless, the angry, the jealous, the outgoing, the shy, and even the gay guy. I sure knew how to pick them. And believe it or not, all but one professed to the Christian faith. As you've probably guessed, I have some stories to tell! But I'll get to those in the coming chapters.

I've wanted to write this book for years because I have felt so strongly about not compromising or getting married just to be married. And now that I am wed, I feel like I have the credibility to share my dating stories of lust and love, loss and lies, restoration and redemption, and ultimately, the realization that he is truly worth the wait!

At thirty years old, I finally had the confirmations I'd prayed for. I knew Kevin was the man who would be my husband. But I had a lot of failed nothings before I met him. And through those painful processes, I learned the important lesson of not settling or compromising.

How? It came down to accepting peace. I don't mean the sort of peace that just accepts defeat. It's an inner peace that flows from the depths of your being after you choose to surrender your heart and desires to the Lord.

By sharing my stories and what I have learned, I hope to give you some tools that will help you find that inner peace. I'll share my journey of overcoming loneliness in singleness and how I did so. And I'll show you practical ways you can surrender and submit yourself more and more to our loving Father.

We'll talk about the importance of remembering that you won't be perfect, your future spouse won't be perfect, and life won't be perfect. But we serve a perfect Savior who can take our inadequacies and turn them into something beautiful.

And hopefully you'll also come away with a greater understanding of your own mindset and what's important to you in a prospective spouse. During my times of dating, it was always consternating trying to determine why something bothered me about a relationship. I had to put my beliefs and expectations under a microscope and really examine them.

When I was hurt or disappointed, I had to figure out not only what I was feeling, but *why* I was feeling a particular way. I had to essentially become my own psychologist; digging into the *why* helped me determine what beliefs and characteristics were most important to me in a future mate. That discovery always led to experiencing more peace. And oftentimes, it was because that meant saying goodbye to a wrong relationship.

After you delve into the why of what you think, feel, expect, and believe, you will be equipped to create healthy boundaries for yourself. These are emotional boundaries to protect your time and heart. These are physical boundaries to honor God, your body, and your future husband. And these are spiritual boundaries to keep your relationship with God first. Cultivating boundaries in singleness will create healthy habits and spiritual disciplines that will set the groundwork for a solid, God-honoring marriage.

The biggest, most daunting question while dating is often,

How do I know if he's *the one?* I have heard so many philosophies about whether or not there is a "one," a "true love," or a "soulmate." I'd even heard one of my professors at a Christian university say that we shouldn't bother the Lord by praying about trivial things such as what house to buy or the person to marry. I nearly fell off my seat!

My God loves it when I come before Him with everything in me—all my worries, concerns, hopes, and dreams. And that includes not only who I dated but who I married. If He counts every hair on my head (Matt. 10:30), then he certainly cares about the man I marry.

But what about all the people, like the professor, who don't believe in that? Well, "you do not have because you do not ask" (Jas. 4:2 NKJV). I believe it comes down to faith. If we don't ask in faith, why do we think we will receive?

If you believe God has set aside someone who was created to be your helpmate, then pray *in faith* for him; and in God's timing, your faith will be rewarded.

How do we know who that man is? We have the best resource right *inside* of us. All we have to do is ask for the Holy Spirit's direction, and He will be faithful to give it. We just have to choose to follow His gentle prods.

It comes down to seeking after the *perfect will* of God. Yes, He will permit you to live a happy life with a Christian man of your choosing. But think of how much more amazing it will be to marry the man whom God created to complement you perfectly, a man who seeks God's face first, a man who will empower you to follow more passionately after Christ, a man who will love you like no one else on earth can. Think of how much more you can accomplish for the kingdom of God in that sort of marriage!

So live your life. Live it wholeheartedly, with passion and excitement.

And in the waiting, let the fruit of His Spirit become one with your spirit. Let the love of Jesus transform you from the inside out. His love is more passionate than a thousand lovers. It's more ardent, more fervent, and more relentless than any earthly love that chases you. And the peace you feel will be more lasting. The joy, more fulfilling. The excitement, more exuberant.

And as you wait, you'll learn to wait in patience, in expectation, and in trust, allowing you the freedom to truly live and enjoy your life and not wilt from wishing away your singleness. You'll learn to embrace this gift as a time to prepare your heart and follow God with full abandon, committing your time and life to Him.

If this time of singleness is a gift, then it's a gift to offer the Lord, wrapped in love and devotion, an offering of the most precious thing you can bring—your everything—joyfully surrendered to the King!

# BREAKUP AFTER BREAKUP

You must think breaking up is what I do best—
I let guys go like some people change their clothes.
My brother rightfully dubbed me
queen of the first date.
I can say—
"No, but thanks for the grub, Bub,"
and "Well, that was a good show, Joe"—
without a worry that whichever
big-talkin', odd-smellin', goofy-lookin',
pot-smokin', sailor-swearin',
unimpressive dinner date fate brought me today
was no knightly prince charming.
But there's so much you don't know
about my letting go . . .
The last guy I dated was an ill-fated setup—
a dinner/movie date.
Now he's just another name
to cross off my list of prospective kids.
But I don't always say goodbye so heartlessly.

You thought I dumped you like an old pair of shoes.
But you were my favorite shoes
that just didn't quite fit, but I didn't want to lose.
So I'd dig them from the ditch where I had dropped them,
dust them off, or dry them out, and try to fit them on again,
only to remember why I had discarded them,
and then, I'd let you go again.
But of all my goodbyes, breakups,
good lucks, and no thanks,
only one hurt like the fire
of a branding iron—
that seared your mark
forever on my heart.

# Chapter 1

## KNOW WHAT YOU WANT

Imagine throwing yourself into a river in an effort to learn how to swim. If you haven't learned what a breaststroke or backstroke is, how to float, and other basics of how to swim, you'll be swept away with the current. Like swimming, if you know "the basics" of what you are looking for in a dating or potential marriage partner, you won't sink at the first wave (or un-matched gentleman who comes your way). We'll look at gauging what basics you are specifically looking for so you can more easily navigate and wade through the waters of dating.

I've heard it said that finding someone to marry is not finding what you need, but finding what you want. And that is because you shouldn't *need* a husband. Know who you are without a man first. If you are confident in who you are, then a man won't feel the need to have to complete you, because that's a lot of pressure. Just as you wouldn't want the stress of a man feeling dependent on you to complete him, a man also wouldn't want you to need him to feel whole. Instead, two independent people coming together can complement each other in a beautiful and healthy way. Would you want to feel the weight of having a man who needs you to complete him because he would be completely lost without you, or would you want a man who is so confident in who he is in Christ that it fosters that confidence inside you?

For me, the process of knowing what I wanted in a man started with knowing who I was first. And who I was didn't take shape immediately. It was a process. In my time of singleness, I grew closer to the Lord and turned to Him for my needs. And it was through that turning that I realized He was the only One who can and should handle the weight of all my needs. Putting that on a human isn't fair.

It was also during this time of putting my trust in the Lord that I discovered who I was. I realized that I wasn't the shy, insecure girl I had been as a schoolgirl. I was an independent, confident woman who knew who she was and what she wanted in a man. And I wasn't afraid to say goodbye if I discovered the man I was dating wasn't who I wanted.

I think it's important to point out that I wasn't confident in the way society views confidence. It wasn't the cockiness of thinking I deserved the world. Rather, it was after constantly putting my trust in the Lord that my confidence in the Lord grew. And soon, I was confident in who I was as a daughter of the Most High King, who could conquer anything the world threw at me with Christ before me. I was confident that I was competent to do anything the Lord put before me because I knew He wouldn't give me anything I couldn't handle. And I knew I wanted a man who was strong and confident in the Lord too.

I wasn't independent in the sense that I didn't want or need anyone else and insisted on going it alone. But I was independent in that I would go wherever the Lord directed. I wouldn't put all my dependence on one person. Instead, I would trust Christ in me, the hope of glory, to direct me. And it was because of that independence that I did something I never would have considered before—I became a flight attendant in April 2013. And during the last seven years of flying, I have had so many adventures and met so many interesting people. My life has been touched in more ways than I can even count because of the vast number of people I've met who have influenced my life. And I can hope that I've influenced theirs for the better as well.

The further I went in this journey called life, the more I grew to put my dependence on God. And the more I depended on Him, the more I came to the knowledge of who I was on the inside. And once that happened, I knew what I wanted in a spouse. Though it wasn't until I started dating that I learned more and more of what I *didn't* want in a spouse.

You'd think as a Christian gal, I would have found a nice selection of Christian men. I recall regaling stories about ex-boyfriends to a fellow flight attendant once while we were killing time during an all-nighter flight. After realizing all the crazy stories I had, I said, "You name it, I probably dated it." As I mentioned at the beginning, I really knew how to pick them.

Through each failed attempt at finding someone suitable, I was able to add something to my list. When I was twenty-six, after breaking up with my first boyfriend, I created a list of two sections: *Must-haves* and *It'd be nice.* The must-haves were nonnegotiable. And that's where I found my deal breakers. The more guys I dated, the longer that list became. It was from that list that I created questions to ask dates to see if I wanted to even bother getting to know them further. The question that probably shocked the guys the most was if they had any gay tendencies. But then I would explain the backstory to that one.

Unfortunately, guys, like girls, can lie. And sometimes when you put a guy on the spot, he won't be as forthcoming as you would like. He will try to make himself look better and possibly skirt around uncomfortable questions. So you have to assess not only what he says but how he says it. What's his body language saying as he's speaking? Is he making eye contact? Is he shuffling in his seat uncomfortably?

Sometimes you won't know he's lied until you catch him in the act. I once asked a guy if he swore. He answered no (since he knew I didn't cuss). But then after hearing him around the corner, swearing like a sailor with his friends, not only was I disappointed that we didn't have that in common, but he immediately lost my trust and respect. And two particularly important things you need in a relationship are *trust* and *respect*. So if a man has lost them both within the first several dates, there is no need to continue.

I always made certain guys knew up front that I wasn't out to play games. I value honesty very highly, and I would rather they hurt my feelings but give me an honest answer. The truth is always best because, one way or another, the truth will eventually come out. And the longer it takes for the truth to surface, the more that lie is going to hurt.

This philosophy goes both ways. It's best not to cover up things about yourself that you think he won't like. It's best to be open about it from the get-go. Because if he doesn't like whatever it is, he isn't worth your time to begin with.

You have to be able to accept each other. As human beings, we can change little things about ourselves because we should be ever growing and maturing, but we shouldn't try to set out to change monumental things about another person. If we can't accept each other from the start, what makes us think that will change? It takes an awful lot of pride in oneself to think we can change something about a person who's been a certain way for as long as they can remember.

I don't say these things to make you too picky. (Although I was told more than once that I was being too picky.) By having a template, so to speak, we know the groundwork of the type of person we want. The "big picture" of who they are. And if you find someone whose big picture, hot-button items are in agreement with yours, there may be something there worth pursuing. Because if we only have little quibbles (rather than deal-breaker items), then little differences are less significant and can often easily be rectified. Bottom line: You won't find someone who is exactly like you. So if you can make peace with minor differences while embracing the larger similarities, you'll be off to a great start with having a successful relationship.

## My Waiting Story

My first kiss was from my first boyfriend at age twenty-five. I had told him he had to know he wanted to marry me to kiss me. So after five months (which was my longest relationship until I dated my now-husband), he kissed me. But I wasn't attracted to him in the way I needed to be. He wasn't bad looking by any means, but I didn't have that physical chemistry with him. When he gave me my first kiss, I wanted to be excited; yet I couldn't help but feel disappointed. *What is wrong with me?* I wondered. Wasn't it supposed to be butterflies and fireworks? Instead, I was grossed out by the weird squishiness of his lips and the slobber he left on my chin.

I remember being asked by friends if it was difficult now that we had started kissing to refrain from going further (since we were saving sex for marriage). I was frustrated by how often I got the question. No, it was not difficult at all. I didn't have any inclination to go further. I did want to keep kissing him, though, because I kept hoping that something inside me would click and I would suddenly enjoy it. But that never happened because you can't manufacture chemistry.

Yes, I thought he was good looking (attractive). But chemistry is more than just finding a man physically attractive. Rather than simply one person admiring another, it involves two people.

It starts as a back-and-forth spark, and ignited by mutual interest, it can go beyond the physical appearance of a person. Then it can grow into an even stronger connection of chemistry through interactions over time.

## My Waiting Takeaway

After that failed first relationship, I started making a list for things I wanted in a future husband. Notable items that made it on there in addition to being a believer were: he can't be a liar or be addicted to alcohol or pornography. With someone addicted to alcohol and pornography, being a liar comes with the territory. Again, it came down to the fact that I just knew I had to be able to trust the man I would marry. Without trust, any prospect of chemistry is destroyed. To have chemistry, I determined that the man couldn't have a propensity of lying. With my first boyfriend, my heart sank each time I learned of a new lie. Each was a little devastation that caused his attractiveness to diminish. He was a handsome man by the world's standards; but each unsavory detail unearthed made my admiration fade. That is because there is a direct correlation between character and how we perceive their levels of attractiveness. If we admire a man's character, chemistry grows. Chemistry speaks to the attractiveness of the heart. Increased feelings of chemistry will make physical characteristics more appealing.

So please, don't keep dating someone you're not attracted to. Even if they have all the qualities you are looking for, but you don't find that person attractive, then you won't ever gain chemistry with them. And that means no matter how hard you try to muster or manufacture attraction or chemistry, the relationship is just never going to work. You need both facets to weather any storms you may face in the future.

## Your Waiting Step

Try writing a list of things you consider nonnegotiable items you want in a husband. Also, add a side list of things that you don't have to have but would be nice. And then bring those lists before the Lord and pray for your future husband and specifically for those things you've listed.

My husband and I have compiled a couple of potential lists to give you some ideas of where to start for your own lists. Take a look at these ideas and then spend some time making a couple of lists of your negotiable and nonnegotiable characteristics. Keep in mind that these are things you are listing to bring before the Lord in prayer. Allow Him to shape your lists and shape your heart with His desires for qualities of your future spouse.

*Must-haves*

- God-loving/God-fearing
- Honest
- Straight
- Shared theological standpoints
- Financially responsible
- Doesn't have a criminal record

*It Would Be Nice*

- Number of children wanted
- Open minded
- Loves animals
- Physically active
- Safe driver
- Has good relationship with his family

Now, these are just ideas to help get you started. There are so many options to consider that may or may not be important to you. So here's a list of things to think about. You can decide if any should go on one of your main lists.

*Options to Consider: Yay or Nay?*

- Drinking?
- Gambling?
- Drugs?
- Smoking?
- Porn?
- Tattoos?
- Foul mouth?
- Video games?
- Traveling?
- Time conscious?
- Political views?
- Introverted or extroverted personality?
- Likes/dislikes animals?
- Loves worship?
- Enjoys the outdoors/hiking/camping, etc.?
- Entertainment preferences (TV shows, music, etc.)?
- Food preferences (Italian, American, Chinese, Mexican, etc.)?
- Has/wants children?
- Has dreams and aspirations?
- Friendly or flirtatious with other women?
- Plays an instrument?
- Into competitive sports?
- Likes board games?

This isn't an exhaustive list of ideas, of course. And things that I would put in my lists may be different from what you would choose for yours, but this should help give you a start.

The Lord was so gracious with me when He gave me a husband who not only meets every criterion on my *Must-have* list, but he even meets everything on my *It'd Be Nice* list as well! Only by the grace of God did that happen. There are even characteristics my husband exhibits that aren't on my lists that I didn't know I would want that complement me perfectly.

Just to give some examples of things on my secondary list to give you a reference, I wanted someone who liked cats, since I love cats. And after dating a guy who was allergic to cats, not having cat allergies went on the nonnegotiable list, since I had a cat. And my husband not only wasn't allergic and loved cats, but he also brought a cat into our relationship. And both our cats got along splendidly from the start.

I also hoped for a man who was a musician, since I am a violinist. And sure enough, I got a husband who sings and plays the trombone. And after we got married, we joined our church's worship team together, which is a joy I never imagined before.

However, sometimes I would shift items from one list to the other. I always thought it would be nice to have similar food preferences. But I soon realized that if I wanted to be able to cook for my husband and him for me, we had to share similar tastes. And as the years went on, I moved it to my nonnegotiable list. I couldn't imagine having to make two separate meals every night to accommodate both of our likes. And then adding children to feed into the mix someday just was too much for me to consider. Guess what happened when I asked my now-husband what his favorite foods were? Yes, they matched mine very well. We have minor differences, of course, such as his love for sausage, tomatoes, and rosemary, none of which I can understand. But he doesn't understand my love for cilantro, beets, or cold medicine either. Thankfully for us, those were extremely minor differences and easily remedied.

Still, food preferences and dietary restrictions are important things to consider. Because even your food allergies will affect each other. I am lactose intolerant, and my sweet husband refuses to even have any regular milk in the house so that he won't accidently bake with it. So we have Lactaid milk, lactose-free ice cream, and lactose-free cream cheese and sour cream. Yes, these are all more expensive, but he doesn't want to risk giving me an adverse reaction that will affect the rest of my day.

If your potential spouse has specific dietary restrictions, it could be beneficial to try adjusting your own eating and cooking to see if you can also be on that diet too. It will make cooking for each other easier, and they will greatly appreciate your sacrifice.

Of course, that's not to say my husband never eats dairy, but he's conscious of the fact that I would love to eat dairy just as much as him. So if he is going to eat a dessert that I can't, for example, he'll make sure I get a dessert I enjoy that I can eat too. I should insert here that he did learn the hard way at a family birthday party where I got my feelings hurt when he ate cake in front of me that I couldn't have and there was nothing sweet lactose-free that I could eat. But then I felt guilty for making him feel bad, because I knew I should be happy for him that he was enjoying a treat.

Ultimately, relationships are about putting each other first. And I think that's the biggest reason we get our feelings hurt—when our spouse does something that makes us feel like they don't care. Marriage is a continual reminder to put our spouse first. I think dating is a good place to practice this. We can easily slip into the thought pattern of, why bother since we aren't married to the person? The reason is because you may *eventually* marry that person, and the habits you make while dating will carry into marriage.

While practicing putting your boyfriend first is wonderful, if he isn't making it a practice of putting you first, there may be a problem. We don't want a one-sided relationship. Now it could be that no one taught him to put others ahead of himself. Or it could be that he is selfish. If it's the former, there is a chance that nudging him in the right direction may help. But if it's because of the latter, it may be because of self-centeredness, or perhaps that he isn't as interested in you as you are in him. Regardless, if that's the case, you may want to consider that your current relationship doesn't have future potential.

Marriage is a constant cycle of giving and receiving, and if there is only one giver and one receiver, that circle is broken. And soon the giver will want to stop giving, and then the receiver will become upset at the giver. Instead, it should be a constant flow. But we shouldn't keep score. Keeping score only invites disappointment and feelings of unfairness. The fact of life is that sometimes when life is good, we will give more; and other times when life gets us down, we will receive more. That's the beauty of a self-sacrificing relationship. You are there for your spouse no matter what, love them no matter what, and will give of yourself no matter what you may receive in return.

Ultimately, when you are determining what you want in a husband, flip the card and recognize that he will want the same qualities in you. Strive to be like the person you want to marry, and when your paths do cross, you will find yourself better prepared for marriage than when you were simply on the hunt for the perfect man.

### Your Waiting Journal Tips

Whether or not you've begun either of your lists, here are some questions to ponder and journal. What is the most important thing I am looking for in a spouse? Do I also reflect that characteristic within myself? If not, are there practical ways I can become more of the woman I want to be? Pull out your journal and take a few moments to jot down some thoughts after reading this chapter.

**Verse and Prayer**

"O Lord, You have searched me and know me. You know when I sit down and when I rise up. You understand my thought from afar. You scrutinize my path and my lying down, and are intimately acquainted with all my ways. Even before there is a word on my tongue, behold, O Lord, You know it all. You have enclosed me behind and before, and laid Your hand upon me." (Ps. 139:1–5 NASB)

*Father God, You* know me better than I even know myself. You count every hair on my head. Please help me grow closer in my walk with you. And I ask for guidance as I ponder the type of man I would like as a helpmate. Lord, guide my thoughts as I create these lists. And I pray that You will ultimately allow Your will be done in who I marry. I give You my hopes and dreams and ask for You to mold them and shape them into Yours. Make me like clay that I can be fashioned into the sculpture that You find pleasing. I want to glorify You in everything I do and say. And I want to give You the authority to lead me—whether that is to the mission field, to a friend, to a husband, or to a new calling—I give You permission to guide me through this life. In Your precious Son's name, Jesus. Amen.

# EMPTY SPACES

We fill each day with either work or play. And when we have free space, we quickly fill it with TV, sports, friends, coffee, breakfast, lunch, or dinner dates. Because we don't like empty space—that space between to-do lists and prior engagements. That unmarked time between workdays that still needs to be filled.

But I started to wonder why? Why are we so afraid of silence? Is it awkward . . . to be both in public and private without our phones, music, or headsets?

The answer is yes. I even find it awkward to sit in my own house in silence.

But I see now how empty space is powerful. I was unexpectedly sitting in silence, and I realized: it wasn't so bad.

In fact, it was inspiring. So I started to write.

I started realizing how filling my days, hours, even minutes only distracted me from what my heart really wanted: to spend quality time with my Creator, my lover, friend, and constant companion. Even when I'm busy contemplating my to-do list of cleaning, laundry, packing, shopping—oh yes, can't forget to take the cat to the vet or change the sheets before leaving for the Laundromat.

But the moment I stop the chaotic mayhem of doing things, my brain decides to remind me of other things that need doing.

And then I return to my reflections on the only One who can help me relax and keep from taxing my body and brain from this constant need to be doing something.

And I start to realize that I don't have to *do* anything but simply *be* with Him because I don't have to prove anything to Him. He accepts me without prerequisites. His only requirement is that I rest in Him. And He abides in me. No striving, just relishing His presence, which He gives without partiality.

Whether we're acting in our weakness or strength, He remains the same. He won't remove His presence simply because we're being immature or imperfect. He knew our flaws when He accepted us, and He freed us from our imperfections the moment that He saved us—because now all He sees in me is the perfection of Christ.

I know I'm a work in progress, but knowing that He sees me blameless gives me the boldness to live with the single-mindedness of pursuing Him and His righteousness.

And in consequence, I pray to gain the confidence to not fear the silence, but instead to create empty space to dedicate to pursuing His presence . . . and to simply sit in silent awe of Him.

# Chapter 2

## YOU WON'T BE PERFECT

Nearly every diamond has an imperfection or inclusion. But that doesn't make it any less beautiful to the naked eye. For centuries, women have loved diamonds for their beauty. But guess what? You are like a diamond—beautiful and imperfect. Only Christ is the perfect diamond without spot or blemish.

It's okay to be a work in progress. It's okay to falter and get back up again. The key to remember is to always try again and ask the Lord for His help and for His perfection to work through our humanity.

Although I knew that no one was perfect, I honestly thought I would be as close to perfect of a helpmate as one could be. That could have been partly because I grew up with very encouraging parents. Or perhaps it was because the guys I'd dated thought I was the bee's knees (until I dumped them). Or perhaps it was because of my easygoing nature. But what I hadn't realized was that I was easygoing with friends or even prospective spouses because I had the mentality of, *Well, it's not as if I'm married to them.* And that mentality works well with friends because you aren't going to have the exact same philosophies and beliefs as your friends. And that's okay. You aren't married to your friends.

Even with dates, I didn't push disagreements by broaching subjects we disagreed on. Instead, when I discovered a disagreement that was a deal breaker, rather than trying to change their minds, I would simply break up with them. Clean. Easy. There was no need to start an unending argument over something that I knew would ultimately end in our relationship's demise.

That didn't keep me from bringing up controversial issues, though. I wanted to know early on if there were any potential disagreements on things that were hot topic issues for me. So I didn't shy away from asking questions. But I did shy away from arguing about those issues if I could help it. Making a clean break was easier.

Because of this habit I had formed, I thought I was an excellent communicator. Whereas many of my friends would find it difficult to ask their boyfriends the important questions, I would ask right away, "Do you want kids?" or "Are you addicted to anything? Video games? Porn?" And that is also why I'd had so many short-lived relationships.

Unfortunately, I wasn't quite as excellent a communicator as I assumed. Just because I could bring up uncomfortable topics did not mean I could easily communicate when a miscommunication had occurred. And in marriage, miscommunications are bound to occur.

Once I married my best friend (who also happens to be my little brother's best friend), I realized my error. I wasn't going to be a perfect wife. And I wasn't even an excellent communicator. Yes, I knew how to communicate. But I didn't always know how to communicate *well*. It's important to learn conflict resolution when dating because it's a vital skill to maintain a healthy marriage.

I could communicate in a way that I could understand. But it was another thing entirely to communicate in a way that the male brain could understand, and in a way that was respectful to my husband. I never had to deal with long-term communication. And I never experienced having to work out issues until they were resolved. This was a relationship in which I couldn't just jump ship. And of course I didn't want to, but that meant figuring out how to resolve miscommunications and issues in a way that was understood, received, respected, and resolved. I soon learned that was a tall order.

Husbands apparently can't read minds. They also can't read between the lines. And they can't guess thoughts based solely on your body language, exasperated sighs, or your silence, nor can they tell what you are feeling when you aren't even certain how to describe your feelings. And I soon realized it was foolish to think that my husband would be able to do these things.

Even after I opened my mouth to communicate, I found that the words I used were not increasing his understanding of why I felt the way I did. Simply saying how I was feeling wasn't always enough. I had to figure out *why* I was feeling that way. If I was feeling hurt, I had to analyze the root of the hurt—not only what prompted it but why it prompted it. Truth be told, I have gained a greater understanding of myself through this introspection. And I hope that you also realize that although it's completely normal and okay that you aren't perfect and don't communicate perfectly, it's helpful to practice effective communication when you're dating because it prepares you for marriage. It will make life much easier when you get married if you've learned those skills during the dating phase.

**My Waiting Story**

My first married argument with my husband is a prime example. . . It was a few months after we had tied the knot. We were right in the middle of the summer heat, which in Oregon meant temperatures in the nineties during the day. My husband had come home from work. As a manager of a grocery store, he would often come home with a few things that we needed from the store. I was always appreciative of that since not many wives can say their husbands willingly go grocery shopping.

So this particular evening, he brought a bag of groceries inside, and we ate dinner that I had made. The rest of our evening went by nicely as we enjoyed one another's company. But then, as we were preparing to go to bed, I asked him, "Did you happen to buy some milk?" since I remembered him saying he would get some, but I couldn't recall seeing him put it in the fridge with the other grocery items.

My husband froze. "Oh, no."

"It's okay if you forgot. I can get some tomorrow." I thought that would be the end of it.

But my husband put on his shoes hurriedly, saying, "I didn't forget it. I just forgot to bring it in the house." And he ran out to retrieve it from his car in the driveway.

He came in and put the milk in the fridge.

I frowned. "We're not actually going to drink that, right? It's been sitting out in a warm car for four hours."

He nonchalantly answered, "It'll be fine. I did the face test."

"What is the face test?" I asked, somewhat incredulous.

"I put the carton to my face, and it was still cold enough. We do it at the store all the time."

Again, I was shocked. "You do this at the grocery store? What about temperature checks?" I knew the frustration was showing in my voice, but I felt like I was making up for the lack of emotion he was showing as he acted like nothing was amiss. Couldn't he tell I had a problem with this?! Nope, he couldn't read my mind. So I was going to help make certain he knew I was not okay with drinking potentially rotten milk. "Well, I hope you don't expect *me* to drink it."

"No, you don't have to drink it." His answer was abrupt as he seemed to finally catch on to the fact that I was upset. Raising his own voice, he countered, "I'll drink it!"

"Fine, you drink it." I let out an exasperated grunt.

"Fine, I will!" And he quickly poured himself a glass of milk right there.

"Well, sorry for loving you and being concerned about your health." I still had a little edge in my voice, but now the hurt was evident.

He set his glass down. "What do you mean?"

Softening a little too, I answered, "Growing up, you know my dad would fix kitchen equipment in restaurants. And he would always check temps to see if the food was in the safe zone or not. And because of his work, at home he always erred on the safe side. 'When in doubt, throw it out.' He said it was because our health was more important to him than the few dollars he was throwing away."

Understanding dawned on both of us as my husband realized I wasn't reacting because I was upset that he forgot the milk in the car, but I was reacting because I thought he didn't care about my health.

Though we are two different people with two different upbringings that we bring to the marriage table, we have to find a way to communicate what we are thinking and why we are thinking that way—even if the reason why is because of a mindset that formed twenty years ago.

It was my turn next to feel for my husband, because our milk conversation was not over yet. After he apologized for making me feel like he didn't care about my health, he said, "I felt like you were attacking me as a grocer. I told you that we do the face checks at work, and you acted like that was ridiculous."

It was my turn to apologize and reinforce in him how much I respected the work he did and what a great leader he was. After which, my husband then admitted, "I know the milk was out a long time, but I was embarrassed that I forgot to bring it in. I didn't want to let you down. So I guess my pride got in the way. I'm so sorry."

Now that right there, honest to goodness, is what my husband said. I know most men aren't able to articulate their thoughts and feelings or admit to their man pride. But the Lord knew I needed a man who could communicate. So somehow He blessed me with a husband who could explain his side of the story in a way that brought me down from my high horse of having to be right and helped me realize that we both had preconceived notions that led to our misunderstanding.

We immediately embraced. It may seem silly to cry over milk that wasn't even spilled, but we cried together. It was our first argument, and we were so thankful that we recognized quickly where each of us was coming from in our hurt. And most importantly, we didn't go to bed angry.

## My Waiting Takeaway

I will admit though, although I wasn't angry, I went to bed a little hurt. My husband is not one who easily raises his voice, and that was the first time I had seen him so upset that he raised his voice a bit. And even though I also had raised my voice, he quickly forgave me and was able to go right to sleep. I couldn't understand it.

I think perhaps as women we hold onto hurts longer. So I had to spend a lot of time in prayer that night, asking God to forgive me and also asking Him to help me forgive my husband for hurting me in turn. After an hour or so, the Lord gave me the peace I was hoping for, and I fell right asleep.

Marriage isn't the end. I hope that by getting a glimpse into my first year of marriage, it is evident that marriage isn't perfect. I am not perfect. My husband isn't perfect. And whoever you marry will not be perfect. But we strive to live at peace with one another, love each other, show respect and kindness, and also try to understand where the other is coming from. The more we learn about where we are coming from in a situation, the closer we feel to each other. The same principle can be applied to dating. It just becomes amplified in marriage.

An unfortunate belief propagated by our society and media is this notion of *happily ever after* once a couple gets married. And on the other end of the spectrum, we then have this widespread acceptance that marriages will end in divorce—and that the man is stereotypically one way, while the woman is another, and they can never make it work. Both are absolute lies.

Addressing the latter first, yes, men and women have propensities toward behaving in certain ways; but that doesn't mean that all men and women fit in those boxes, and it also doesn't mean that they can't come to understand where the other is coming from. There have been countless times in our marriage that my husband and I have discovered that a hurt was rooted in a simple misunderstanding. The reason: men and women communicate differently. But that doesn't mean we should call it quits and find someone else.

That brings me to the notion that once we get married, we will live happily ever after. That is also a crock. A man and a woman living together will have disagreements and misunderstandings. The key is to communicate effectively what those are and respect each other's opinions. And then you will grow closer to your spouse. I know firsthand how much it means when your spouse spends time listening to you to understand where you are coming from.

And I've seen how much it means to him when I listen to him to understand him better.

There is good news here, though. Marriage doesn't always have to be a struggle. It doesn't have to be endless disagreements and misunderstandings. Marriage can be absolutely magical when two people enter into it with their hearts and minds open to each other. And then you'll be walking along in awe of a brand-new world, full of the unknown, mystery, and excitement. Everything is a new adventure, and you have an amazing adventure partner who is experiencing it all with you.

That is, if you wait for the partner who is right for you. He might show up when you're young, or he might show up when you're old. You might be wondering, How do you know who is right for you? Only you can answer that question. But my hope is that by sharing my stories of trial, error, love, and loss, I can help you better answer that question for yourself.

## Your Waiting Step

Accept that you are not perfect, and that's okay because no one is. But realize that you have a perfect Savior who lives inside of you. The embodiment of perfection lives inside of you. All you have to do is ask Him for help, and He is ready and able and excited to be more a part of your life.

## Your Waiting Journal Tips

Think about ways where you may feel inadequate. These may be general characteristics or ways you worry you may fall short as a wife. You don't have to write them down if you don't want to. But write the Lord a letter where you are giving Him all your worries, concerns, shortcomings, and failings. Ask Him to take anything in your heart that makes you may feel unworthy and replace it with His love.

## Verse and Prayer

"We all stumble in many ways. Anyone who is never at fault in what they say is perfect, able to keep their whole body in check." (Jas. 3:2 NIV)

*Lord, I know* that You are the only One who is perfect. You are perfect in every way. Where I fall short, I ask that You cover the distance to make up for my lack. When I fall, I ask You to hold me in your loving arms, brush off the dirt, and help me stand again. And I ask that You will help me in my pursuit to live more like You. Make me more and more into the image of Your Son, Jesus. I pray that You will make me into a wife someday who follows fully after You and puts You first. Guide me to be a great helpmate to my husband. And if You have prepared for me a life of singleness, allow me to be a wonderful helpmate to friends and family around me. In Your wonderful name. Amen.

# RECKONING HEART

She pulled the icy sheets to her chest, shivering.
Increasing the heat couldn't shake the chill.
Curled in a fetal ball, she lay shaking,
certain the coolness not only touched her skin,
but also came from deep within.
How could she stay warm with half a heart?
In leaving him, her heart split in two—
it was like a butcher knife
piercing the soft flesh of her chest,
plunging deep, slicing and separating
her heart that was weak, barely beating,
broken, and bleeding.
But each time she stubbornly decided
not to remove the blade,
she stepped deeper into the spider's web,
snuggled in the silky hammock—a seemingly safe place to sleep—
unaware of the spider lurking, patiently waiting for her
to give in to the siren call of sleep . . .
Finally looking up from her self-imposed thorn in the flesh,
she saw Someone standing behind her.

His eyes were alight and kind,
His face empathetic and beckoning,
His hair glowing and golden,
with hands cupped in front of Him.
At her curious glance, He opened His hands,
revealing a heart, healthy and whole.
She thought of her own tattered heart
while staring at the complete heart in His hands.
Hardly a fair trade.
She knew if she kept her eyes on Him,
she could remove the blade.
But she feared the sudden sting
of a gaping slice in her heart.
Yet in reaching out, she realized
He knew well of holes—
Nail scars
marred and made beautiful—
As His outstretched hands
Embraced her new heart.

# Chapter 3

## LONELINESS

Sometimes being alone but not feeling lonely can be a difficult feat. But it's one that can help us grow. Rock climbing, for instance, is something you can do alone. Every step higher, you grow in perseverance, strength, and stamina. But you aren't truly alone, as you have a harness to catch you if you begin to fall. And that harness can be symbolic of God's protection that will cradle and catch you if you lose your footing. So no matter how high the climb or far the fall, that harness will be there if we took the time to secure it before the climb. Taking time with God beforehand will never be for nothing. Every moment spent with Him tightens the strength of His protective harness as we rock climb through life.

During my time of singleness, I experienced many times of loneliness and even jealousy because I was missing out on a life that it seemed everyone else got to have but me. As I mentioned earlier, I got married at thirty. So I had experienced thirty years of singleness. Many of those years I watched my friends, acquaintances, and coworkers get married and start having children. I know what jealousy feels like. You may also relate to the dichotomy of feeling excitement for your bestie's engagement while simultaneously mourning your own singleness.

For me, I tried to console myself with the thought that I was traveling and experiencing so much excitement on my own. It was true. But it didn't stop me from wishing. I would often process my thoughts and emotions through writing, especially poetry, and I would surrender my doubts and uncertainties to God. He was the One who gave us emotions, and there isn't a single emotion we bring before the Lord that is going to startle or shock Him. He loves us so much and is so glad when we bring our hearts before Him.

Through my praying and writing, I was able to grasp a greater understanding of what I was going through. I grew in my walk with the Lord, I began to rely on Him more, and I turned to Him for the companionship I so deeply craved. And I pray you grow in that sweet companionship with the Lord, because you also can learn to appreciate those times of loneliness because of what it produces in you.

## My Waiting Story

Sometimes it didn't matter if life felt fly or if I was going through a storm. Regardless of the weather, I faced the ugliness of loneliness popping in on me from time to time, sometimes letting it overstay a welcome it should not have had. It crept in on me and slowly became my companion. But loneliness often brought its friends: brokenness, hopelessness, despondency, and depression.

I would blame my loneliness on the fact that I lived alone in my little studio apartment. When I first became a flight attendant, I was new to the town of Medford, Oregon. So I felt that my loneliness was acceptable because it was understandable since I didn't have friends or family nearby.

I can remember loving the independence of living alone but hating the loneliness. Yet no matter how much I loathed it, like a cathartic medicine, loneliness became my friend and reminded me of my emptiness. This constant reminder fed my dependence on selfishness, self-pity, and self-indulgences.

And when I got stuck in the cycle of pitying myself, I forgot about anyone else. I found that as I gave in to the loneliness, all I could see was *my* loss, *my* fear, and *my* pain. It stained everything I saw with images of me—color blinding me from everyone else.

You know how it is when someone is talking and you're trying to listen, but all you hear is your own inner voice taking over the dialogue? It's like color blindness. I can't see the color blue when it always looks green, so try as I might, I was still pretending I could see the blue hue of someone's eyes—when I couldn't. Why? Because the size of my loneliness had encompassed all my senses.

No matter how hard I tried to exit that highway of the royal I, me, and mine, I couldn't because loneliness is close friends with selfishness. And when you stay friends too long, it's hard to leave their companionship.

On top of the loneliness, another thing that had always scared me about living alone was that I might choke and suffocate when swallowing one of my vitamins. No one would know or be there to help. That may sound like an irrational fear, but several years ago, it happened.

A big vitamin C had lodged in my throat—too far down to come back up, but too far up to go down. I started guzzling water, but the C refused to be forced down. It simply wouldn't budge. I started having trouble breathing and realized that I would probably have to perform the Heimlich on myself. So I looked around the room for something to lean against. Then my gag reflex kicked in. With the first compulsion, all the water I'd downed came hurling through my nose and mouth, unfortunately spewing onto the bed. But by the fourth heave, out popped the vitamin!

## My Waiting Takeaway

Although I could have very easily assumed that the situation with the vitamin C only validated my biggest fear, it didn't. Instead, I realized that if we choose to put our trust in the Lord, then even when we think our fears are coming to pass, He will save us from them all.

So how did I overcome spiritual color blindness and change my attitude to that of gratitude that the Lord had saved me? I had to accept spiritual glasses. The only way to overcome the color blindness of selfishness, loneliness, and depression was to overhaul my perceptions. Though I had 20/20 vision in the natural sense, I suffered from nearsightedness in the spiritual sense. I first had to accept that I couldn't see further than myself before I could accept the divinely crafted, God-given glasses to correct my limited perceptions.

Through surrendering my loneliness to the Lord, it was an instant cure. But it takes a lifetime to maintain—especially when I feel tempted to take His glasses off again. I need to remember to ask for His perspective so I can see through His lenses.

Spiritual drowsiness and apathy was always a precursor to loneliness that would creep in. But like they say, it's okay to not be okay. It's just not okay to stay not okay. What I constantly learned about loneliness was that by choosing to stay in that state, I was choosing selfishness. But if I could recognize and accept that I was feeling lonely, surrender my feelings and emotions to God, and accept His companionship, then the selfishness had to leave because I stopped focusing on myself and started focusing on God. Yet whenever I was tempted to remove the lenses, I had to identify who the author of temptation was and remind myself where my heart and treasure reside.

## Your Waiting Step

If you've been waiting a long time for the right person to come into your life, I hope to encourage you. You aren't alone in your loneliness, but more importantly, you aren't alone because your Father is right there with you, waiting for you to turn to Him for comfort. So if you're feeling lonely, your next step is to turn your heart to Him. He wants to be your comfort, your companion, your Forever Love.

I know turning to God for comfort isn't always easy, but it's always the best option. And it's more than just a quick prayer. Surrendering our will for His will looks different for every person. But many times for me, I remember being alone at home with worship music playing, while on my knees, crying out to God for comfort. Perhaps you've been there too. Sometimes we don't know what to say, which is why I strongly encourage turning on worship music. You'll be surprised how just the right song will come on at just the right time. Or perhaps turn on a sermon or a podcast—something that will direct your eyes heavenward. As you turn to Him, Christ will be waiting to engulf you in His loving embrace.

As a now-married woman, when I'm feeling down, no matter how long my husband holds me, his touch cannot take away even an ounce of my anxiety or pain. I can tell you that as amazing as it is to have the physical warmth of your husband's arms around you, you won't find true, lasting comfort until you know what it is to feel the all-encompassing embrace from your heavenly Father's arms.

Feeling the embrace of the Father is just the beginning because you are already complete by the Savior of your soul. But many times, we choose to revert that completeness to the man in our lives. Yet if you put that kind of pressure on any man to make you feel complete, you will never feel satisfied. But by placing your complete dependence on God, you will have confidence in Him.

And if you are a confident woman in Christ, you can then encourage confidence in the man you're dating, and later your husband. You have the freedom to encourage them in the Lord, and they will in turn encourage you.

### Your Waiting Journal Tips

When you start to feel lonely and start to feel the selfish gimmies, jot down some options to help you through, so you don't have to stay there long. If you are an inner processor and have a propensity toward writing, then journaling, blogging, and poetry can be an outlet for you. Perhaps you're a verbal processor and need to audio record or video record your thoughts, which could assist in your coping with what you're thinking and feeling and help you understand what you're experiencing.

Are there any physical places you can go that will inspire a sense of community? What about online places, like Pinterest, you can visit to help inspire you as you work through your thoughts and feelings? Whose number do you have on speed dial who will encourage you when you need it? In addition, write down the ways you feel closer to God. Is it through worship music? Prayer or soaking in His presence? Scripture reading? Or hearing sermons?

Whenever you feel lonely, draw close to the One who helps you not feel lonely, whether it's someone in your life or your heavenly Father—and hopefully both, because we need each other to continue pointing us to Jesus.

### Verse and Prayer

> "As iron sharpens iron, so one person sharpens another."
> (Prov. 27:17 NIV)

> *Lord God, that* is what kind of relationship I want
> to have: one where I sharpen the character of my

someday spouse while he simultaneously sharpens mine. But in the meantime, I pray that I will be an iron to sharpen those close to me and that they in turn will sharpen me. I ask, Father, that You cover me with Your loving arms. Surround me with Your presence when I feel loneliness encroaching on me. I want to thank You for Your amazing love. Thank You that because of You, I never have to feel alone. Amen.

# SURRENDER

Surrender is not about striving.
It's about submitting and relinquishing my will.
I can only see the smallest part in the larger picture of
life.
Perhaps if I could glimpse the future,
the present decisions would be simpler.
But since I don't know what's forthcoming,
I'll choose to live by faith—
forgetting what's behind and pushing forward to what's
ahead,
to what Christ has in store,
surrendering my will for His,
and in the process, succumbing to the most splendid,
stirring love—
a love that surrendered everything for His beloved.
As the shards of bone and glass beat His body repeatedly,
He endured blow upon blow in agony
and took tormenting torture willingly,
pouring out His lifeblood sacrificially.
In the most breathtaking, overwhelming goodbye,

He forgave me for forsaking Him.
And the moment I renounced my rejection of Him,
He destroyed the separation between us,
giving me admittance to His presence
and bestowing upon me His tender affection and eternal passion.
How can any earthly thing compare
to His unyielding, undying love?
How can we not sacrifice
something that cannot last
and will not bring happiness
for His loving kindness?
How can we not forsake the flesh
and forgo temporary indulgences,
when we consider the eternal gift
of the contented joy and bliss
Christ offers for this very moment?
So I lay down my selfish desires,
and I allow my will to come into submission
to the authority and Lordship of Christ,
giving His will permission to purify and pervade
every circumstance, situation, and every aspect of my life.

# Chapter 4

## DON'T SETTLE

In the Bible, Abram's wife, Sarai, was barren for a long time. In her impatience to have a child, she told her husband to sleep with her maidservant, Hagar. Abram did; and Hagar bore a son named Ishmael. That's what Sarai wanted right? Now her husband had a child from Sarai vicariously through her maidservant, but Genesis 16:4 says Sarai grew to despise Hagar.

In addition to being barren, she has envy to contend with, as her husband bore a son through her servant. She didn't know God was planning on opening her womb when she was an old woman. She didn't know she would then conceive Isaac. Sarai acted out of impatience because she couldn't see the full picture of her life.

And the consequence of that didn't just affect her and her own jealousy. It affected two entire people groups—the descendants of Ishmael (Muslim people) and the descendants of Isaac (Jewish people)—who would later go on to despise each other as generations of fighting have ensued. I don't think either people group can imagine what life would have been like had Abram and Sarai waited patiently for God to provide them a child.

## My Waiting Story

At nearly twenty-eight years old, my biological clock was ticking, and I felt like I was getting old. I knew I wasn't an old maid by current standards, but I was a decade behind when my mom married my dad. When I was in high school, I wondered how on earth she married so young since I still felt like a kid. Plus, at that point in high school, I'd never even been on a date.

But as the years passed, I learned I didn't want to be stuck in the cycle of loneliness I easily had fallen into. I realized I could actually be satisfied with my singleness. I had to come to the conclusion that moping in loneliness and self-pity was not living. So I made the conscious decision to not let loneliness drive me, and I decided I wouldn't settle in relationships anymore. Little did I know that in just a few years, I would be at the altar saying "I do."

I learned that everyone is on their own path, creating their own timeline, story, and legacy. I know it's cliché to say, but I had done many things in my singleness that I wouldn't have done had I married early.

I traveled, for instance. I can guarantee that I wouldn't have become a flight attendant. Traversing the skies and calling it work has been the most exhilarating, trying, exciting, frustrating, beautiful years of my life. I have undergone more trials and triumphs in those first years flying than I potentially faced in all my other years combined.

For instance, I had trouble staying healthy. Those first years of being in a metal tube filled with recycled germs took a toll on my immune system. I was not only sick a lot, but the pressurization of altitude changes often caused a simple cold to turn into a sinus or ear infection. And that meant being off work for the seven to ten days it took to heal on antibiotics. And even antibiotics stopped being effective as doctors changed up the types of antibiotics they prescribed.

I also had my fair share of heartbreak. When I experienced the pain of heartbreak or illness or discontent or loneliness, I desperately desired to see a change in my life. I wouldn't trade all those hard experiences. Not for a simpler road. Not for the complacency that accompanies an easier way, because when life emerges as we expect it to, according to all of our scheduled plans, apathy can naturally take root.

Back to being twenty-seven. After a few failed short-term relationships, I found that I was content, even though I hadn't come close to finding someone who was right for me. I could almost say I didn't care. I appreciated my singlehood because I was beginning to see how every season in life was fleeting. So I wanted to cherish the time and opportunities singleness afforded, like the opportunity to get up late and type away on my laptop because one day I could be busy with the responsibility of children. And each time I'd end yet another relationship that had turned into a short-term nothing, well-meaning well-wishers would say the typical trite sayings.

*"You're going to find someone amazing because you're amazing!"*

If I had a penny for every time I heard that one during my single years, I'd be a rich woman. Even though the sentiment can seem banal, I often appreciated it, because at times, it was easy to start believing that all the amazing guys really had been snatched up.

Instead I would respond with, "I'm trusting the Lord with that."

*"You'll find someone when you're not looking."*

Another overused suggestion. I think it's safe to say that most singles aren't actively looking (unless you're doing online dating). That is, until you see someone who catches your interest, at which point, you may pursue an acquaintanceship with said individual to see if it could be a potential match. But more often than not, it's not, and that's okay.

But what do you say when someone says that? I used to say, "I didn't think I was looking," or "Next time I'll try not to look." These answers seemed to pacify the well-wishers.

*"There's no timeline, so don't feel rushed."*

With this one, I would just be honest. "Sometimes it's hard to not feel rushed as I'm getting older."

To which they always replied, "You're still young!"

"Well, thank you for saying so," I would always respond, even though internally I felt the struggle of not feeling young anymore.

Every time another relationship ended, I realized I was at square one again. And starting over meant a lot more time. That also meant my biological clock would relentlessly keep ticking.

I have always wanted children. Even now in marriage, I still want children. It's much like trusting the Lord for a husband—I have to keep trusting even after we've had heartbreak after heart-break, miscarriage after miscarriage. I have to put my desires fully into His capable hands. It's a continual surrender because constant fear likes to try to slide in undetected.

In dating I learned the importance of continual surrender and surrendering my desires to the Lord, and I continue to feel the stirring of its importance in my soul. I genuinely believe that He wants us to always be in a state of surrender to His will.

Surrendering to Him doesn't mean you won't find your spouse early on; that just wasn't my personal story. I marvel at the fact that some people find their spouses so soon in life. I dated a lot of frogs. Unfortunately, a frog isn't your prince, and kissing him won't make him a prince. By that I mean that continuing to date someone who doesn't share your values won't magically change him into some-one who does. I've always had the mentality that you shouldn't try to change him. Certainly compromise on insignificant things, but keep in mind you can't change the person he is. If you can't accept each other when you're dating, then you probably aren't suitable for each other.

## My Waiting Takeaway

Through the tests and tribulations, and in feeling my faith go through the fire, I learned about and saw perseverance and character develop in my life; and most importantly, God could be glorified through my growing. When I learn from my shortcomings, He gets the honor. And when I struggle, I seek His face with all my strength. When I fall, He picks me up. When I overcome, He rejoices with me. When I succeed, He beams with love for me. Regardless of what season I'm in, He stays with me, and He gets all the glory.

Breakup after breakup, I soon realized that I wasn't going to compromise what I wanted in a husband for the sake of getting comfortable in a relationship. And I also realized that until I found someone who wasn't a compromise of my values, I was satisfied living alone with my cat (which sounds startlingly like a crazy cat lady statement). Still, I loved traveling the skies, sleeping in new places, and then getting to come home and cuddle with my kitty. It was a time in my life that now, in retrospect, I would never trade for anything.

## Your Waiting Step

If I could impress just three simple things on you, my dear reader, they would be: Choose Christ. Choose life. Don't settle.

### Choose Christ

Choosing Christ first is something you will never regret, because He can help you overcome the loneliness. How do you choose Christ? You choose Him every time you spend time with Him, reading His Word, worshipping, praying, and soaking in the beauty of His creation. You also choose Him every time you let a prospect go who you know won't lead you closer to the Lord. You choose Him every time you say no to temptation (whether that is physical temptation to sin or emotional temptation to stop trusting the Lord in something). Whenever you are tempted, just remember who the tempter is. And remember that Jesus too was tempted, but He overcame. And with His help, you too can overcome anything the enemy throws your way!

### Choose Life

To choose life means that you are not wandering around aimlessly, waiting for your knight in shining armor to arrive. You can choose to live your life to the fullest! What are things that bring you joy? Perhaps singing, dancing, sports, music, reading, or writing? Do those things. When you choose to live your life, it will give you exciting stories to tell your future husband one day. And trust me, he will smile adoringly at you as your face lights up telling him all the things that you are passionate about.

### Don't Settle

Not settling is going to look different for everyone. It means, don't allow your impatience to lead to compromise. Don't feel forced to wait. Choose to wait. You may think the right one won't ever come around or that he doesn't exist. I thought that very thing so many times. But by not settling, I allowed myself to live a wonderful life. I always said, *I'd rather be happy and single than miserable and married to the wrong person.* And I was happy and single. (I was only miserable during times when I was either dating the wrong person or when I gave in to loneliness.)

So please don't settle for someone who might be the one, or

someone you want to make into the one. Don't settle if you have determined that all the good ones are gone. Instead, trust in the Lord and live your life. Because when His timing comes, your husband won't be perfect, but he will be so worth your patience.

You may be wondering—what about people who never marry? Some people are called to lives of singleness, and I believe God gives grace for that. But some people wish away their entire lives, hoping for prince charming to come riding in. And then they are too busy looking to realize life has passed them by and they missed out on so many joys in life available to them.

So I want to clarify that when I refer to *waiting*, I mean to wait patiently. Don't try to make your will become God's will. I've tried that. Believe me, it doesn't work. Dating the wrong guy longer, trying to make him into the right guy, only adds to your own heartache or his when you finally do let him go.

In your waiting, if the "right man" never comes and you end up being single for the rest of your life, living a life dedicated to Christ, loving Him with everything in you, giving Him your first and your best without any distractions, then rest assured, He was also worth it. You may be thinking you've spent your whole life waiting for a prince to come; all the while, you've grown closer and closer to the Prince of Peace. And once your life comes to a close and you enter into the presence of your One True Love, I wholeheartedly believe you will look upon His glorious face and realize: *He* indeed was worth the wait.

### Your Waiting Journal Tips

Journal about what patience means to you. What does it mean to wait patiently? And in what ways can you focus on your relationship with God first before concerning yourself with finding a marriage partner?

**Verse and Prayer**

"And why are you worried about clothing? Observe how the lilies of the field grow; they do not toil nor do they spin." (Matt. 6:28 NASB)

*Lord, You know* me and all my anxieties. Thank You for blessing me and taking care of all my needs. Even though I cannot see the full picture of what my life will look like, I trust You. If You clothe the lilies, how much more will You take care of me? I want to put my heart and trust fully in You. Help me not make decisions out of impatience.

Please guide me in this life to be patiently waiting for the plan You have for me. I ask for you to give my future husband patience as well, as he may also be feeling impatience. Please give us both Your inner peace. And Lord, if You have prepared me for a life of singleness, then give me single-hearted devotion for only You.

Let me not be swayed by the temptations of the world to settle. I ask for the divine gift of patience in waiting for whatever You have in store for me. Thank You. In Jesus's wonderful name. Amen.

# ALL IT TAKES

Your name on my screen
startles my heart to fluttering.
Will I ever let go?
I convince myself each time
that this time is the last time—
just one more chat, one text, one word
before I say goodbye.
Just once more swapping photos
and sweet sentiments,
while I fondly gaze at your immobile face
frozen on my screen.
After hours of catching up elapse
and words begin to slow,
I feel so
exposed and
left with raw emotion—
bliss-filled moments intermingle
with heaviness
as my languishing smiles become
anguishing aches.

Desperate desire stirs
from the depths of my soul
as I type:
I miss you.
I stare at those words we share so often.
I feel so selfish—
stealing your attention,
knowing I must return it.
I feel so selfish—
as my hungry heart
collects your compliments
like a squirrel storing nuts
for the winter season.
I feel so selfish—
longing for you like I do,
wishing I could give up
part of myself
so we could be together
again.

# Chapter 5

## KICK SHAME IN ITS LYING FACE

L et's go back to the diamond analogy. We determined that diamonds are insanely valuable to us even though you would be hard pressed to find a perfect one. Even though imperfections are there, it's only under a jeweler's intense magnification that they can be seen. Well, think of yourself as the jeweler, because in focusing on your inadequacies and therefore feeling shame for them, you use that jeweler's magnifying glass to blow up your imperfections so much that you cannot see past them. But there's great news. Christ sees you for the diamond that you are, and He makes you perfect through His blood. So remember that the next time you are tempted to focus on your history or on your imperfections. All inclusions have been sealed up by the healing blood of Christ, and shame has no place in your redeemed life.

Every human being on the planet has dealt with shame in one way or another. If you're alive, you've felt guilt. But if you've been adopted into the family of God, then you can put shame in its rightful place and out of your life.

Maybe you've read up to this point and think that you don't deserve to wait for someone worth waiting for. Let me tell you right now, that's a lie from the enemy! Perhaps you didn't wait in the past. Perhaps you've given yourself completely away or had a failed marriage. Perhaps you're struggling with the guilt of not feeling worthy of a worthy man. But remember, you have been redeemed! You have been set free from the bondage of sin. If you have accepted God's salvation, then also accept that He sees you as clean—a new creation, washed in the blood of Jesus. You are pure and white, and your past is forgotten.

Yet shame wants to keep you bound and wants you to believe you don't deserve good things. But you are free in Christ Jesus, and you are free to live in abundant freedom. You are free from sin through the power of His Spirit.

I too have experienced shame rear its ugly head. Shame doesn't care if what you experienced was your fault or not. It just wants to keep you down. And it doesn't matter if you feel shame from your own behavior or because of someone else's because the Lord sees you as faultless.

We have to accept Christ's forgiveness, and by accepting forgiveness, we are also renouncing our right to hold certain attitudes such as unforgiveness, bitterness, or hate. How can we accept forgiveness when we haven't forgiven someone else? I think that acceptance of forgiveness is often something we will continue to accept through the rest of our lives, as we live in continual gratitude for His grace as it covers our past, present, and future mistakes.

## My Waiting Story

In the past, I have dated guys who tried pushing the boundaries I gave them. It seemed like a game to one—to see how far he could go before I stopped him. Since I didn't know what was coming, I didn't know the times I was about to be groped and wasn't able to always stop the anxious hands in time. I struggled with shame from that. Not only because it was an injustice, but because of my own inability to stop it.

Some from an older generation may be shocked that the suitors in question were Christians. I only ever dated one nonbeliever (a story I'll get to later). But in fact, these were Christian men who professed Christ on Sunday and then tried to push my boundaries on Monday. I really had to grapple with that, and when I couldn't reconcile that being right, I would end the relationship.

I remember confiding my frustration to a Christian gal from church. She said something that proved to be true: "Christian or not, a man is still a man. In a marriage, you want a man who can lead you spiritually. But in dating, you need to set the precedent for the physical relationship because he will go as far as you let him."

Even when I was dating my husband, who is a godly man, once we started kissing (after eight months of dating), we had to continually have discussions about *exactly* what our boundaries were. Giving each other backrubs was previously fine but eventually became off limits. It wasn't an issue before we started kissing, but soon after, backrubs became much more of a turn-on. And we accepted that we'd stop giving them. We did allow neck rubs, which was helpful since we both frequently had knots in our necks. Since neither of us had ever experienced sex before, we didn't realize that when we were turned on, our bodies naturally craved each other because we were craving sexual intimacy.

## My Waiting Takeaway

I now have a philosophy that the best way to preserve yourselves and save you both from extra temptation is to not even kiss before marriage. Before you call me crazy, hear me out. I think kissing is a beautiful expression of love. And trust me, I know how intense that desire is to kiss the one you love. But once my husband

and I started kissing, that's when we had to add boundaries and readjust them when we got too close to breaking them.

For me, I wanted to make sure I liked kissing him before we got married because after that first boyfriend, I'd always been paranoid that I'd fall in love with a horrible kisser, although a big part of that was simply that I didn't have chemistry with my first boyfriend. But let me tell you, chemistry has not been a problem with my husband and me. Thankfully, we only had to wait about six months after we started kissing to get married. It would have been difficult to wait much longer.

After we got married, we discussed that if we could do it over, we would have set stricter boundaries in our dating relationship because we wish we could have preserved every bit of the newness of the experience for marriage.

But to be clear, we aren't sitting in shame bemoaning our past. It is just that—in the past. Psalm 103:12 reminds us that our sins have been removed as far as the east is from the west. If you think about it, the east never actually touches the west because the east is so far from the west that neither ever reaches the other. And if Christ doesn't see our past mistakes, we shouldn't keep looking back either.

## Your Waiting Step

Think about what you want your physical boundaries to be in a dating relationship. Without clear boundaries, it's a setup for ending the relationship with regret and pain from going farther than you meant for it to go. Uncomfortable as it may be, you need to set exact boundaries so you both know where the line is. And if you inadvertently go a little farther than you wanted, discuss it immediately. Don't push it under the rug and just think it won't happen again because it will if you don't redefine your boundaries. By determining what you feel is appropriate and what isn't when you're in the dating phase, setting healthy boundaries will help you and your future spouse in the long run.

Yet even in our boundary setting, we all fall short of what we hope. Every human does. So when we fail, the key is to acknowledge that we have stumbled and refuse to stay in regret, bemoaning our past mistakes. Living a life free of shame starts with your mindset and surrendering your mind to the Lord.

What do physical romantic boundaries look like for you? When you're dating, it's good to remember you are getting to know an imperfect person. And just because they made mistakes in the past, it doesn't have to define who they are. Granted, if you are with a person who has a history of unfaithfulness, then chances are unfaithfulness could very likely be in their future.

It's good to still use discernment and listen to the Holy Spirit in regard to someone's character. And if their character proves to be unhealthy, it might be healthy to let them go. Even though Christ forgave them, and you can forgive them, it doesn't mean you have to marry them.

Everyone's story is different, so ultimately, listen to the promptings of the Holy Spirit. Once you know you've met the match that He approves of, tie the knot, say "I do," and get ready for a great adventure!

**Your Waiting Journal Tips**

In what ways have you let shame influence your thinking and actions? Are you behaving in certain ways because you are letting past shame influence your present life? Think of any shame you may have, wrap it metaphorically in a gift box, and offer it up to the Lord in exchange for His forgiveness and love. As you do this, allow the Holy Spirit to minister to your heart, then write down what you feel He is impressing on you. Let Him shower you with love and joy.

## Verse and Prayer

"We all, like sheep, have gone astray, each of us has turned to our own way; and the Lord has laid on Him the iniquity of us all." (Isa. 53:6 NIV)

*Thank you, Lord Jesus*, for dying on the cross, taking away all of my sin and iniquity! By Your grace I am saved and set free from sin. I praise You for Your forgiveness. And I ask right now that You will change any shame-based-mindsets I may have and turn them into heavenly mindsets. I also pray for my future husband in this area and ask that if he has fallen into any sin, please deliver him out of it speedily. I pray You will protect his mind and heart during this time. And I pray that You will bless him mightily and give him peace. In Your awesome name. Amen.

# YOUR WIDE-OPEN HANDS

Today I lay my heart on a platter,
then closing my eyes and holding my breath,
I place it in Your wide-open hands.
Standing anxiously, I wait to see
just what You'll do as I release
every single part of me.
Through the mist, I see You
grasping my heart with infinite care
as You gently pull it into Yours.
My heart is captured and overtaken,
enraptured and overwhelmed.
I am hopelessly lost, desperately dazed,
ardently devoted, as I stand amazed—
simply captivated by the grace of Your face
and by the intensity of Your striking gaze.
Yet suddenly I start to question myself.
I question my hopes and dreams,
and soon I'm questioning everything.
I see the strings of my heart
separating from Yours as I pull the cords,
seizing my heart back into myself.

Oh, what have I done?
Break the ties I've made
and bind me back to You.
I surrender myself again,
relinquish my grasp anew,
and release my heart and will to You. . .
Today, I laid my heart on a platter,
then closing my eyes and holding my breath,
I placed it in Your wide-open hands.

# Chapter 6

## FRIENDS AND FAMILY

Balancing time with friends and family while engaged in a new dating relationship can take diligence to maintain. Think of it as regular car maintenance. Imagine everyone in your life as a vehicle. It takes work to keep a car running—you must continue adding fuel so it never depletes, change the oil regularly, and monitor the internal temperatures and brake fluid and tire tread. In a new dating relationship, it's easy to do this.

But it takes intentionality to make sure your keep your friend's and family's gas tank/love tank filled. You need to spend time with them to monitor the temperature of your relationships to keep them at healthy levels. If you don't spend time with them, then you won't notice when their oil runs low and the engines/relationships burn out.

When dating, it's sometimes easy to make the whole world revolve around that special person. He's suddenly the center of your universe, and everything and everyone else fades into the background. While this is only natural, it's important to remember to not completely neglect your friends and family, because if that relationship doesn't pan out, who are you going to go to for comfort and support if you've burned all your other relationship bridges?

I know various relationships can be hard to balance. Before your special person showed up, your life had a rhythm and flow that was normal to you. When he made his entrance, everything changed, and it's difficult to know how to prioritize, except that seeing this person is so intoxicating that you want to spend all of your time with him.

Your church or your parents may be pressuring you to set boundaries in dating, which may feel frustrating to you. And if people who love you are imposing dating restrictions on you and your beau, it probably feels like they are saying, "We don't trust you." But here's the thing. Remember, they have been exactly where you are now, and they know from experience just how strong temptation can be. That's why they want to keep you from making the mistakes that they did and keep you from the regret that follows. Or, if they waited, they know how beautiful and special the marriage relationship can be when you wait.

Here are some ideas I found helpful when trying to balance friends and family with your significant other when dating.

## Group Gatherings with Friends

Have double or triple date nights with married or dating friends. Or if you don't have friends who are married or dating, then have game or movie nights with your single friends. And if both you and your significant other don't have the same friends, have events where you can invite both your friends and his friends so that everyone can get to know each other. Doing this will help all of you bond together, and it will help your friends not feel neglected. Plus, you'll still be spending time with the one you can't stop thinking about. Everyone wins!

*One-on-One Meetings*

If the big group scenario doesn't appeal to you, perhaps you'd prefer this idea. Get together with your love interest and one friend at a time. The intimacy of one-on-one time will allow each friend to feel like they were given the special opportunity to get to know your man and to give their approval of him. They will feel valued, and it will only strengthen your relationship with your friends.

*Family Dinners*

Have your date over to family dinners. This will allow your family the opportunity to get to know him as well. If you are too embarrassed to have your family meet him, you might want to rethink whether this relationship actually has long-term potential.

Something to remember about your family: They will give their input whether you ask for it or not, and that's not always a bad thing. Sometimes family sees things about our relationships that we do not because they are outside the relationship. We may not see clearly through our rose-colored glasses to know when something isn't quite right.

Of course, you need to consider the source when accepting your family's input. Does this family member love the Lord? Do you trust and value their opinion? If so, take what they've said before the Lord and ask Him to reveal the truth to you.

**My Waiting Story**

I value my parents' advice because they love and honor the Lord and listen to His voice. In the past, there wasn't a single gentleman I brought over to whom they gave their wholehearted approval. It was consternating. When I was in my late twenties and still couldn't find a guy my parents wanted me to marry, I just thought they didn't consider anyone good enough for their only daughter. But I waited, and when I started bringing Kevin around for the first time, they were completely on board with my relationship.

## My Waiting Takeaway

Having my parents' approval was not only further confirmation that Kevin was the one for me, but it was vital to me. Knowing that they loved the Lord dearly and listened to the Holy Spirit, I craved their yes of approval because it confirmed that I was hearing the Lord too with a strong affirmative answer.

## Your Waiting Step

Marriage is too important a decision to simply marry someone you *think* you can make it work with. It's too important to simply marry someone because you want to be married. And it's too important to marry someone because you think it will be a fix-all for whatever problems you two may have in your dating relationship.

Get input from those close to you whom you respect. Not everyone has parents who love the Lord, and if you don't, I would strongly recommend finding someone (a godly couple in the church or your pastor) you can go to whom you trust and respect and who will give you an honest opinion of the person you are with.

Your friends are also good resources for you to gain insight into your relationships. But choose wisely whom you listen to, because even your friends may be biased or may not be completely honest with you because they don't want to put their friendship in jeopardy over a guy, or perhaps they aren't following the Lord. In these cases, weigh carefully the things your friends say.

Of course, when a true friend who seeks after the Lord comes to you in humbleness and tells you that they don't have a good feeling about the man pursuing you, this is someone you should listen to and take what they say to the Lord in prayer.

Since deciding whom to marry is such a monumental decision,

second only to choosing to follow Christ, you should consider carefully what those close to you have to say. Weigh everything they say with Scriptures, and then weigh it with what you are hearing the Lord say. Because when it comes down to it, you need to hear the Lord for yourself about whom to marry.

## Your Waiting Journal Tips

Brainstorm a few ways you would like to incorporate a future boyfriend into your circle of those close to you. If you have been in past relationships where you neglected friends or family, what will you do differently in the future to protect and nurture those relationships as you develop a romantic relationship with your significant other?

## Verse and Prayer

"Greater love has no one than this, that he lay down his life for his friends." (John 15:13 NIV)

*Lord, allow my* love for my family and friends to grow so strong and enduring that I would lay my life down for them. Please grant me the wisdom to have good solid friendships with those You have for me. Help me be a good friend to them, and allow me to marry someone who respects my close friends and family. And may my family and friends wholeheartedly give their blessing on our union. I put my full trust and belief in You, with this and with all my needs and desires. Thank You, Jesus, for Your faithfulness. Amen.

# THROUGH TEMPTATION

TEMPTATION can start as a push-pull,
back-and-forth between the head and heart.
When I know that what I want
is not what I need,
I try to believe that I need what I want.
I thought I'd ended my torment
when I ended our unequally yoked relationship.
But just because we weren't dating
didn't stop my heart from hanging
onto the memories, meetings, messages.
The mental merry-go-round
caused me to drown in dizzy confusion.
This confusion created the delusion
of a false reality that I had come to believe
as the lies detonated inside me . . .
that a little COMPROMISE was okay.
While wondering if he and I could just be friends,
I wanted the benefits of holding his hand
and even hoped that flirting might be permissible
if under the guise of a respectable, platonic friendship.

LIES, like dominoes, are perpetuated on by the previous one,
until pretty soon I can't discern the difference
between the truth of reality and a lie,
between confusion and clarity,
and most pointedly, between love and lust.
We relabel LUST with all kinds of things—
kinship, connection, chemistry.
But underneath the disguises,
its definition doesn't change:
to intensely desire, crave, or covet
that which you cannot have or possess.
Believing the lies propagated by lust
not only impregnates us with poison
but creates a soul tie
that can only be severed by a single act: SURRENDER.
Until we surrender our will,
We'll be held captive by it.
And only in setting down my desires
can I be free from them.

# Chapter 7

## HEALTHY BOUNDARIES

In a culture where everyone is living with boyfriends and treating marriage flippantly, how do you remain set apart? How do you stay true to purity? Let's consider Noah. When God had never flooded the earth before and everyone scoffed at him and told him he was crazy, he continued to build. He listened to God. He obeyed and built the ark.

So when people scoff or laugh or make fun of your standards and boundaries in relationships, continue to build your spiritual ark by spending times of intimacy with the Lord. Listen to His leading in what your boundaries should be. And obey.

In Genesis 6:22, and again in 7:5 (NIV), both verses are the same stand-alone, one-sentence saying: "Noah did everything just as God commanded him." Therein is the key. Complete obedience. When we listen to the Lord, we spend time with Him, drawing closer to Him. That closeness makes it easier and easier to obey Him.

To bring the metaphor even further, while you are safe in the ark—with your boundaries in place—waiting patiently for the man God has for you, time may pass, making you grow anxious as you wonder if you will see the promise fulfilled. And when the rain comes and the storm blows in, others will be washed away in the emotion of their temptations. But you will stand secure, safe, and steadfast in the ark of His protection.

Similarly, Genesis says that the waters flooded the earth for 150 days. I imagine Noah and his family began to wonder if they would ever see dry land again, or if this would be their new normal, living on a huge boat filled with smelly animals and only their family for company.

But chapter 8 says that God remembered Noah. And then He caused the waters to start to recede. Rest assured that even in the midst of your waiting, God remembers you and He sees you and He knows you. He hasn't forgotten you, and He will bring about the promise in His timing.

Not having your boundaries honored before marriage can and very likely will have an effect on your marriage. It certainly did for me. Something that bothered me in dating was that it didn't matter if a premarital boundary had been my own—if the opposing party did not respect that boundary, where was his motivation to follow it? A person is motivated to respect a boundary by *believing* in it. That's when it's shared.

This highlights the importance of dating like-minded men who share your values and boundaries. Through the rest of this chapter, I will be sharing quite a few biblical references that I hope will help you *believe* for yourself that putting boundaries in place is for the best. I know it may seem like I talk about boundaries a lot, but that's because it is something we often need to continue to read-dress. We're human, so we naturally like to push boundaries.

The world of dating is both adventurous and dangerous. My philosophy (weigh it with your own convictions) is that the Lord gave us free will and then placed us in a world where we can choose right from wrong. He isn't imposing His will on us. We must choose it. That extends to dating. We have free will in our dating relationships, regardless of any boundary someone tries to give us. We can choose to do things God's way or the world's, and there is a beauty in free will. Following God can be a struggle sometimes, but there is grace, and there is such a beautiful reward in choosing to surrender to God's way through the struggle. He is so pleased when His children *choose* to follow Him in spite of their selfish wills.

Though it can be a struggle, if you decide to date in group settings, in public places, or with family around, by your own choice, then you are the one choosing to avoid temptation. And the Lord is pleased by that.

Now, you may not have friends and family nearby if you've moved away. And in that instance, you can still date in a way that honors the Lord. And that is where boundaries come in. For example, you and your dating partner can make the collective decision to not kiss until a designated time. Some wait until they are engaged. Others wait until their wedding day. Others wait until a week before the wedding so their first kiss isn't in front of all their friends and family.

Pray and ask the Lord what His time frame looks like for you. Just know the longer you hold off adding any physical touch to your relationship, the easier it will be to avoid the temptation to go too far when you're dating. Perhaps you may even decide that holding hands is as far as you will go before marriage. That is commendable.

For some of you, your unsaved friends might start jeering, as if your decision in waiting for those special moments until marriage is foolish. I also experienced some ridicule when I was waiting. Some insisted that you won't truly know if you enjoy having sex with that person until you try it out. They correlate it to test driving a car before you buy it. I have two things to say about that. First, I dated a guy with a great philosophy on that. He said, "Why would I want a car with a bunch of miles on it? I'd rather be the first one to drive it." I agree with this analogy because if the car (man) has a bunch of miles (sexual experience) on him, then you're going to likely feel insecure and worried about how you stack up with all the other "test drives" he's taken.

Second, the thought of "try before you buy" is connected to a story with my husband. Because we set fairly healthy boundaries before marriage, we had a hard time with the intricacies of intimacy after we got married. You may be thinking, *Ha, that proves the point!* But even though it was a struggle for us, that struggle connected us in a way that may have taken years of marriage to accomplish. Through our frustrations of understanding each other in intimacy, we learned so much about each other, and we learned how to be caring, gentle, forgiving, and tenderhearted.

I treasure those first months because we bonded deeply through it all, and I wouldn't trade those months for anything. And that is why I truly believe you set the groundwork for marriage in dating. If you practice purity when you're dating, then the marriage bed becomes a sacred place of purity and love that goes beyond the physical. It is a bonding of bodies and hearts.

As I'm sure you've determined by now, I'm not in favor of the "try it out first" mentality. If the Lord has made it clear to you that you are to marry that man, then you don't have to worry about how the bedroom will be. That doesn't mean it'll always be easy, because sometimes the Lord allows us to struggle because of what it produces in us as a result. You'll come out of it a stronger person, and you'll have a healthier marriage because of it.

Up to this point, I've only mentioned physical boundaries—which are important—but there are also other boundaries you can erect in your life to prepare you for dating, and subsequently, marriage.

There are emotional boundaries. These are safeguards over your heart so that you can go through dating experiences unscathed.

It's important to protect your heart by keeping your emotions in check. This can be accomplished through regular self-examination and reflection. That means you designate time to take care of yourself.

There are also spiritual boundaries. Although I mention this boundary last, it is actually the most important. Keeping God first in your life will create a firm foundation that the rest of your life can be built on. It takes continual dedication to keep your relationship with the Lord your top priority—as consecrated, precious times that you consider holy.

Ultimately, it comes down to Proverbs 3:5–6 (NIV): "Trust in the Lord with all your heart and lean not on your own understanding; in all your ways submit to Him, and He will make your paths straight." You and your dating partner may not always understand why you're going through something at the time, but if you put all your trust in the Lord and submit to His will, He will make the way clear. And that's not only in dating, but through your entire lives. Even after you're married, you are constantly bombarded with decisions and different paths to take as a couple. Together, you have to put your trust in the Lord, pray for direction, and trust in His leading.

**My Waiting Story**

There was a time when I was dating when my boundaries weren't respected. The first problem was that I had yet to fully define what boundaries I expected my date to follow. I made an assumption that it was early enough that I didn't need to put a physical boundary down yet. So it caught me off guard when he went in for a kiss on the first date. Even then, I didn't speak up—because my next assumption told me he would stop there.

The first thing I learned was not to make assumptions in relationships. The only way a man will know what you're thinking is if you communicate it.

I didn't. And the result was that he let his wandering hands stray to my breasts. I was shocked. No one had done such a thing before. I pulled away but still didn't say anything. He assumed I was uncomfortable kissing so soon, but that wasn't my only issue. It wasn't until the next day that I texted him how uncomfortable his actions had made me. That surprised him because he didn't think he'd done anything wrong.

I went through emotions of shame and guilt and frustration that I hadn't spoken up soon enough. Although I thought I had moved on from the emotions of that time, fast-forward several years. Kevin and I got married.

Right from the start, I had a hard time letting him touch my breasts. I first rationalized that it was because revealing them to someone was wrong for so many years that I couldn't wrap my mind around it suddenly being acceptable now that we were married.

He was disappointed that his touch in that area didn't seem to feel good to me. I continued to try to figure out my unease. Next, I reasoned that perhaps it was just my own insecurities about feeling small in that area. He assured me that he was more than satisfied and found me perfect and incredibly attractive. It was good hearing the words, but it didn't make his touch feel any better.

As time went on, I started to recognize the root to the problem. Even though I had told Kevin about being groped before we were married, I knew I needed to tell him again in light of this revelation to explain why I had trouble with touch in that particular area. Kevin was very understanding when I explained what I was experiencing mentally. Sharing helped us grow closer as a couple.

It also highlighted for me that there was still an issue. The realization that I still held emotional baggage was my first step in being able to work through it and give it up to the Lord. I have now since been completely able to break through the barriers of insecurity and accept and enjoy the love of my husband in this area.

## My Waiting Takeaway

First, I learned to never assume a man knows your boundaries in dating. I also learned it's never too soon to establish your boundaries—not only within your own heart but also to communicate them early to whomever you're dating. I also learned things that happen during the dating season can have prolonged affects, even into marriage.

Marriage doesn't automatically fix anything. If you have any premarital issues or insecurities, marriage only *amplifies* them. Things you may have metaphorically brushed under the rug and not discussed when you were dating will be forced to the carpet's surface later. Why? Because if you treat marriage biblically, then you become literally and symbolically one with that other individual. And that requires great amounts of vulnerability.

No matter how vulnerable you were before marriage, becoming one with someone will require you to strip off scabs and bandages from your past pains and reveal your raw, wounded, open heart to your husband. For your husband to understand who you are and why you behave in the ways you do, then you will have to be completely open with him.

## Your Waiting Step

Consider the importance of being clear-headed when dating. If you make a life-altering decision based on your rosy-eyed infatuation, you may wish you had taken a step back to analyze the situation first. So, how do you stay clear-headed? Create healthy emotional, physical, and spiritual boundaries for yourself and for your dating partner.

### Emotional Boundaries

The Bible says to guard your heart above all else. But how do we achieve this? There are different ways we can focus on being emotionally healthy. We can be mindful of what we're letting into our senses. Our senses are closely knit with our emotions. We can spend time on self-care. And we can set boundaries on our time. Lastly, to fully guard our heart and emotions, we have to set spiritual boundaries.

The benefits of giving yourself these boundaries is that you will be able to stay level-headed and be able to discern what God is saying to you versus what the world is saying. And it will follow into marriage because you will enter into the union being emotionally healthy and better prepared for challenges that are bound to arise.

Without emotional health, we are prone to react out of fear, anger, and distrust. But if our emotions are under the Lordship of Christ, then we will react to challenges with grace, compassion, and desire to understand. "The mind governed by the flesh is death, but the mind governed by the Spirit is life and peace" (Rom. 8:6 NIV).

*Sensory Boundaries*

If we are mindful about what we allow in our senses, then we can keep our hearts pure and better prepared for marriage. Consider what you watch and listen to. Try to be intentional with what you allow into your heart. What entertainment are you allowing into your eyes and ears? Is it edifying, uplifting, and encouraging? Or does it bring you down? Does it cause you to lust or to sin in your heart?

If the latter, consider what boundaries you can make when determining if something is beneficial for you? Think about the types of music you listen to. Maybe depressing love songs or sad country songs only get you down. Likewise, are there certain movies that make you feel icky after watching? Maybe consider looking up movies that have higher ratings before choosing to view them.

Viewing certain movies can desensitize you to violence and sex. It can place unrealistic expectations of perfection on a future relationship. The Bible says "the eye is the lamp of the body. If your eyes are healthy, your whole body will be full of light. But if your eyes are unhealthy, your whole body will be full of darkness" (Matt. 6:22–23 NIV).

Try to prepare yourself emotionally and spiritually for your future husband just as much as you want him to prepare himself for you. This means focusing on your mental/emotional and spiritual well-being as important aspects of your inner self.

### Self-Care Boundaries

Another aspect of having healthy mental and emotional boundaries is setting aside time for self-care. Your mental acuity will be the sharpest when you've taken care of your basic needs. For instance, you can make certain you're getting plenty of sleep so you don't feel run-down during the week. The Bible also speaks to taking care of your body: "Do you not know that your bodies are temples of the Holy Spirit, who is in you, whom you have received from God? You are not your own; you were bought at a price. Therefore honor God with your bodies" (I Cor. 6:19–20 NIV).

Another basic need is taking time to eat healthy. It takes more time to prepare a meal than to grab fast food to save time, but you will keep your body and mind sharp if you sustain it with foods that will truly nurture.

Basic needs are also doing things for yourself that bring you joy. What restores your soul? Go on that hike and breathe in the fresh air. Or take a relaxing bubble bath at the end of the day. Do you like to go on a walk, jog, or run? Work out at the gym? Create some homemade crafts? This is the time to rediscover your hobbies. These are the things that don't feel like work to you because they are rejuvenating and refreshing, and they will exponentially add to your emotional health. There is a profound difference between doing things you love and just wasting time or being busy to pass the time.

Once you get in a relationship and have a healthy grasp of how to take care of yourself, you can encourage your partner in the things that bring him joy and peace. And as two individuals who feel emotionally whole, your relationship will be stronger than ever.

*Boundaries of Time*

Setting boundaries on your time also means giving allotments of time to yourself. If you aren't able to set a boundary on your own personal time, then your schedule will be gobbled up by other things that your friends, family, and your date have for you, which can create potential problems. If you're an introvert, you may want to set aside time to recharge, and if you're an extrovert, you may still want to take time for yourself, because as the saying goes, if you don't take care of yourself, then you won't have anything to give to others. This is time specifically set aside to focus on your own physical, spiritual, and emotional health. Focus on reflection by reading a self-help journal perhaps. Focus on your faith by spending valuable time with the Lord rather than rushing through your day and forgetting about the One who created it.

Obviously, setting limits on time in a dating scenario protects you from going too far physically in a relationship. But you can also put boundaries on how much time you spend communicating when you're apart. This is important because you want to manage your time wisely. To be able to think clearly in a relationship, you need to prioritize your time with and without your date in it.

For instance, if you're working a lot, does he contact you during work hours constantly, or does he respect your time? Similarly, does he allow you girl time when you're out with friends, or does he blow up your phone throughout that time? These are things to consider. And if the answers to these questions is that he doesn't respect your time, then it may be time to communicate with him about your boundaries regarding when it's appropriate for him to be calling or texting you.

If you are intentional about your time, then you can carve out space for time with friends and family so that they still feel valued and important. Maybe you want to take your sibling out for special time together, or perhaps your parents want to spend time with you. What if your best friend is struggling with the idea of not being able to spend as much time with you after you're married? How will you make them feel special during this transition? You don't have to worry about not giving loved ones enough time if you've made it a priority to give them specific amounts of time in your life.

*Physical Boundaries*

This can be the hardest boundary of all, yet there are safeguards to put in place that will help you when temptation comes. We know that temptation starts in the mind because your mind is where you make the decision to give in or not give in to physical actions that might seem innocent but could lead to sexual temptation. If you can make up your mind beforehand to set healthy physical boundaries, then you are better prepared for standing up to temptation. One way I chose to make sure my mind was made up beforehand was saturating my soul with Scripture that convinced me setting physical boundaries was the right thing to do.

*Without boundaries, temptation will be hard to ignore.*

King Solomon warns his son about the dangers of temptation in the following Scripture.

"My son, pay attention to my wisdom, turn your ear to my words of insight, that you may maintain discretion and your lips may preserve knowledge. For the lips of an adulterous woman drip honey, and her mouth is smoother than oil. . . Keep to a path far from her, do not go near the door of her house, lest you lose your honor to others and your dignity" (Prov. 5:1–3, 8–9 NIV). We could just as easily reverse the main character of this verse and say that the lips of an immoral man are sweet as honey, but run from him! If you don't, the Bible says that you will regret it afterward. I think this applies to dating just as much as to marriage. If you don't date God-fearing men, then the immoral man will lead you astray and to regret.

*Without boundaries, it is difficult to honor your body.*

Why is it important to honor your body? The first and most important reason is that God says we should live in holiness, set apart from the way the world lives.

"God wants you to be holy, so you should keep clear of all sexual sin. Then each of you will control your body and live in holiness and honor—not in lustful passion as the pagans do, in their ignorance of God and His ways" (1 Thess. 4:3–5 NLT). If you want to live a life that pleases the Lord, then you will steer clear of sexual sins. The way to do that effectively is to put boundaries in place that will help keep you from giving into fleshly lusts.

*Without boundaries, you may experience physical consequences.*

You should honor your body by living in purity because the Bible warns that there will be physical consequences of giving in to sexual sins. "You will lose your honor and will lose to merciless people all you have achieved. In the end, you will groan in anguish when disease consumes your body" (Prov. 5: 8–9 NLT.) Proverbs is even mentioning the fact that sexually transmitted diseases are a likely physical consequence of disobeying the Lord's command.

The Bible says that our bodies do not belong to us. They first belong to the Lord. The Bible also says, "The wife gives authority over her body to her husband, and the husband gives authority over his body to his wife" (1 Cor. 7:4 NLT). While I was still single, I thought of my body as already belonging to my future husband. If it was for him alone, then I had no business giving my sexuality away to anyone else. And even if I may have thought I wanted to marry someone, I knew that until a wedding ring was on my finger, that man was not my husband.

If you approach dating with this mindset, it will help

you *want* to put boundaries in place. Also, think of how special your future husband will feel when he learns about how diligent you were to protect something that rightfully belongs to him.

*Without boundaries, you may forgo a purity mindset.*

Purity is a mindset, but it's also a lifestyle. The Lord asks us to remain pure in our thoughts and actions. It starts in our minds and is relayed through our actions. Most of all, purity is a way we can demonstrate our love and devotion to God.

"Give honor to marriage, and remain faithful to one another in marriage. God will surely judge people who are immoral and those who commit adultery" (Heb. 13:4 NLT). If we hold to the mindset that we should keep ourselves pure because we consider our bodies as belonging to our husbands even before we have one, then remaining faithful to our husbands starts before we are wed. That also means we can commit adultery before marriage.

Matthew 5:27–28 (NIV) sets the bar even higher: "You have heard that it was said, 'You shall not commit adultery.' But I tell you that anyone who looks at a woman lustfully has already committed adultery with her in his heart." As women, too, we cannot look with lust upon a man who is not our husband to keep from sinning in our hearts.

Even with the bar being set so high, there is such a wonderful hope in the Lord! John 8:7 (NIV) is set right after a woman is caught in adultery and is about to be stoned. Jesus stops them and says, "'Let any one of you who is without sin be the first to throw a stone at her.'" And of course, they all left. None of us is without sin. But there is redemption through the blood of Jesus Christ. And even if you've committed sexual sins in your past or will in the future, don't forget that your sin doesn't have to define you! Let the cleansing power of Christ's forgiveness penetrate through every fiber of your being and restore you to wholeness. Because you have been made into a new creation, set free from the bondage of sin, and made alive in Christ!

There are many passages about sexual sins in the Bible. Why do you think sexual sins are a repeated theme throughout the Bible? My conjecture is that God thinks it's awfully important. And if something is important to God, I want it to be important to me.

1 Timothy 4:12 (NIV) says, "Don't let anyone look down on you because you are young, but set an example for the believers in speech, in conduct, in love, in faith and in purity." So take heart. We are called, even when we are young, to be examples to the young and old alike in how we live our lives. The Lord asks us to be an example in how we talk, how we act, how we love, how we believe, and how we abstain from sexual immorality. Let that be your heart-cry, to lead others by how you live. The Lord won't give us more than we can handle. So if we feel tempted or overwhelmed, we can always pray, asking the Lord for help, and He is faithful and will always give us a way out.

## Spiritual Boundaries

Guard your relationship with God as first, above all else. Jesus said, "Love the Lord your God with all your heart and with all your soul and with all your mind" (Matt. 27:37 NIV). He tells us that this is the first and greatest commandment. If loving God with everything in your entire being is the greatest command Jesus gave us, I think it's awfully important to put safeguards in place to protect that number-one relationship. How do we do that? Consider the boundary of time that I mentioned. Carve out time in your life to consistently spend time with the Lord.

What you do in that time is up to you. Do you feel closest to the Lord while reading His Word? Consider spending time in prayer. Talk to God like He is right there with you. He is your best friend, after all. You can always easily turn on worship music and spend time praising Him for who He is or soaking in His presence. Or you can turn on a podcast or sermon and glean the nuggets of truth that others have learned. Whatever you do during this time, dedicate it to the Lord.

Additionally, it doesn't have to be just during the time you set aside when you talk to God. He loves hearing from His children, and we can talk to Him throughout the day. In doing this, we keep Him in the forefront of our mind and hearts, which is a great place to start in keeping Him first priority in our lives.

*Spiritual boundaries in waiting.*

One key to remember is that in the Bible, the Lord repeatedly asks us to wait patiently. Creating any boundary requires us to be patient and often to wait. Creating a boundary often means sacrificing something we'd rather do for doing something we know we should do.

As humans, we don't always wait the most patiently. But having healthy boundaries will help us be patient in our waiting. Psalm 37:7 (NIV) says, "Be still before the Lord, and wait patiently for him; do not fret when people succeed in their ways, when they carry out their evil schemes." You may wonder why everyone has a boyfriend, fiancé, or husband, but you? Or why do even the wicked have relationships, but you don't? I felt that way too. But the Lord reminds us to *be still* in His presence and wait patiently for Him to act.

When we start to get discouraged, we sometimes need reminders to pray. Pray for your future husband. Pray for yourself. In the stillness, God's peace will come, and in His timing, so will your mate.

*Spiritual boundaries in conversation.*

If you are in a godly relationship, give each other permission to create spiritual boundaries. For instance, allow the other to lovingly turn a conversation's direction if one of you starts to gossip or speak ill of others. You can gently remind him that you don't want to participate in gossip. And he can do the same for you.

Conversation can be an art, learning how to maneuver or direct a conversation in a loving way. We can also not only fall into the trap of speaking ill of others, but also fall into the trap of speaking ill of ourselves. If you notice yourself doing it, remind yourself who you are in Christ. And remember words are powerful. In them are the power of life and death (Prov. 18:21). When your significant other speaks ill of himself, remind him of this as well. Build him up, reminding him of how you see him. If he calls himself a failure in something, remind him that he is successful in every area that matters most—he is a son of the Most High, he has wisdom and strength, and you treasure him.

*Spiritual boundaries create spiritual bonds.*

Agree to pray together and read the Word together. This creates a strong bond in the Lord. "Though one may be overpowered, two can defend themselves. A cord of three strands is not quickly broken" (Eccl. 4:12 NIV). The third strand is the Holy Spirit, who is ever present in a relationship between two believers. Praying together also creates a defense against the enemy, who wants nothing more than to sabotage any relationship built on the foundation of Christ.

Here are some ideas for things to pray about together and pray about separately. Pray for protection for yourself and your significant other. Pray for clarity. Ask that you both will to be able to discern the will of God for your lives. Pray for the full armor of God for you both. You can even insert your significant other's name into this passage when praying it over him:

> Finally, be strong in the Lord and in his mighty power. Put on the full armor of God, so that you can take your stand against the devil's schemes. For our struggle is not against flesh and blood, but against the rulers, against the authorities, against the powers of this dark world and against the spiritual forces of evil in the heavenly realms. Therefore put on the full armor of God, so

that when the day of evil comes, you may be able to stand your ground, and after you have done everything, to stand. Stand firm then, with the belt of truth buckled around your waist, with the breastplate of righteousness in place, and with your feet fitted with the readiness that comes from the gospel of peace. In addition to all this, take up the shield of faith, with which you can extinguish all the flaming arrows of the evil one. Take the helmet of salvation and the sword of the Spirit, which is the word of God. And pray in the Spirit on all occasions with all kinds of prayers and requests. With this in mind, be alert and always keep on praying for all the Lord's people. (Eph. 6:10–18 NIV)

Another good Biblical prayer to use as a prayer guide is written by Paul.

For this reason I bow my knees to the Father of our Lord Jesus Christ, from whom the whole family in heaven and earth is named, that He would grant you, according to the riches of His glory, to be strengthened with might through His Spirit in the inner man, that Christ may dwell in your hearts through faith; that you, being rooted and grounded in love, may be able to comprehend with all the saints what *is* the width and length and depth and height—to know the love of Christ which passes knowledge; that you may be filled with all the fullness of God.

Now to Him who is able to do exceedingly abundantly above all that we ask or think, according to the power that works in us, to Him *be* glory in the church by Christ Jesus to all generations, forever and ever. Amen. (Eph. 3:14–21 NKJV)

What greater gift can you give someone than to pray for them to experience the amazing fullness of the love of God in their life?

**Your Waiting Journal Tips**

Think about ways you can prioritize your time to create healthy boundaries. Pray about what kinds of emotional, physical, and spiritual boundaries you feel God is asking you to implement in a romantic relationship and consider writing them down. Also, consider ways to stay emotionally healthy as you continue to develop a relationship with your dating partner. And lastly, in what ways can you ensure that you keep your relationship with the Lord first?

**Verse and Prayer**

"Because he has set his love upon me, therefore I will deliver him; I will set him on high, because he has known my name. He shall call upon Me, and I will answer him; I will be with him in trouble; I will deliver and honor him. With long life I will satisfy him, and show him My salvation." (Ps. 91:14–16 NKJV)

*Lord God, I pray* that You will help me always keep my relationship with You first and foremost in my life. And I pray that the man I am to marry will also keep You as His number-one priority. I ask for Your guidance as I create boundaries in my life. Show me what boundaries are healthiest for me. And I pray that You will give me the strength and courage to honor them. Thank You for every blessing You have given me. I pray that I won't take Your goodness for granted. Please help me be a blessing to others. In Jesus's name. Amen.

# FORBIDDEN

When he started showing me attention,
he made me smile, laugh, and forget
he was forbidden.
I knew I had no business appreciating
his mischievous smiles and lingering eyes.
But still, his flirtatious interludes left me wanting,
wanting what I couldn't, shouldn't, wouldn't have—
a relationship with someone like him.
So the endless banter continued
until last night when I said, "Stop. Please stop
the endearments, attention, affection."
He said okay and that he knew
he'd never ask me out—
he couldn't, shouldn't, wouldn't,
because it wouldn't work out,
wouldn't be right,
because we're too different,
like night and day, light and dark,
him swearing,
me praying.

his promiscuous past,
my present desire for God.
He said he'd slept with women—a lot of women,
while I sleep alone, always alone—
without regret.
He's consumed by shame I can't take away.
So we ended it there last night,
said sorry to each other
for leading the other on,
ending our silent hoping
for something
neither of us really wanted anyway.

# Chapter 8

## HOW TO KNOW HE'S <u>NOT</u>

## "THE ONE"

et's think of dating like a litmus test. The PH levels in water let us know how safe it is to drink. Though the acidic water won't necessarily kill you, the more alkaline it is, the better the drinking quality can be for your health. Similarly, we have our lists of the type of man who would complement us best; and if we find that type of person, it'll be better for our overall health and well-being to be with them than to be with someone who will be like acid to us.

**My Waiting Story**

Time and time again, the Lord made a way out of a relationship when I found myself in yet another wrong one. I always prayed that He would make His will abundantly clear. I asked for clarity because it's sometimes hard to see His will beyond the starry-eyed infatuation. And other times, we see His will but ignore it because we're having fun dating or enjoying the attention.

*God will make a way out of it.*

I was twenty-two and in college when I first learned the lesson about hanging out with a guy just because it was male attention when I didn't like him in that way. I had yet to go on a date (and I was lonely for male attention) when one day, an old orchestra comrade from my high school days found me on Facebook. He was going to a Christian college, which led me to believe that he was a Christian, which is not always the case.

He started chatting regularly with me over Facebook messenger. I figured chatting online was perfectly harmless. We reminisced about our wonderful memories from high school travels and competitions. It was nice to have someone to talk to after a long day of classes and waitressing.

Soon his messages became more incessant. Until one day, he wanted to get together "to rehash about old times." I was a little nervous to meet with him. Did I really even know him? At the time, I was still underdeveloped in my communication skills, particularly in knowing how to say no. So I agreed and told him that if I was off by eight that night, I would meet him for coffee. But I worked until after closing and tried cancelling.

I was still living with my parents and younger brothers, and this guy (whom we'll call Luke) said he could come over to my parents' house just to say goodnight. I thought that was silly because he didn't know where my parents lived, but he countered that he remembered where they lived. That seemed odd since there hadn't been any reason for him to know where I lived in high school. But in my naiveté, I accepted his answer, told him it was late, and I was ready for bed.

He didn't want to take no for an answer (which should have been my first red flag) after I told him that I had already taken an over-the-counter sleep aid, which I often took to help me wind down after a late night of work. He then insisted it would be a really short visit, just long enough to say hello and goodnight. I finally agreed, and he responded that he was already on his way over.

I quietly knocked on my brother's bedroom door (who was a few years younger than me) and told him what was going on. He was visibly frustrated at my decision to see the guy at nearly 11:00 p.m. I told him not to worry and left the room.

Luke arrived shortly after, and I sneaked out to see him. He immediately gave me a big bear hug as if we had been long-lost friends. We had been classmates, yes, but hardly friends.

After we started chatting, I started to get cold. He suggested we continue our conversation in his jeep where it was warm. The sleep aid was starting to kick in; but again, I complied.

He was just as talkative as I was, and then he suggested we drive to the nearby park because the moon was beautiful. I thought about the cold. But then, as if anticipating my denial, he said I could wear his coat. So again, I was out of excuses, and agreed.

We then sat on the grass of an open field in the park, where we continued to chat mindlessly. I started getting cold again, and the sleepiness was in full swing. So I said as much and asked him to take me back. He ignored the request and kept chatting. I asked him again. And again. He finally acknowledged the question and pleaded with me to stay, insisting that it was so nice being able to talk with me in person.

I was young and naive and had no idea how dangerous the situation was. If he had cared even an ounce about me, he would have taken me home as soon as I'd asked him the first time. In fact, if he had cared about what I had wanted, he wouldn't have even come over. But of course, my sleepy brain wasn't thinking that at this point.

Now well after midnight, Luke kept talking, then started cuddling up close and insisted it was because I was cold. But it made me really uncomfortable because I didn't like him that way at all.

I looked up over to the nearby street and saw someone on a bicycle with a bike headlight. Who would be riding a bike in the cold after midnight? Even from a distance, I made out a shaggy hairstyle that looked just like my brother's and basketball shorts like my brother always wore to bed. Not only that, but my brother was the only person I knew who had installed a light on the front of his bike. "Hey! That's my brother. I told him I was meeting you, and he must have gone looking for me when he didn't see me return to my room! You have to take me back—*now*!"

He begrudgingly complied.

I ran back into the house as quickly and quietly as I could and peeked in my brother's room. He appeared to be sleeping. So I surmised that he had arrived home before me and gone back to bed.

I spent the majority of that night writing Luke about why I didn't want to see him again. He kept arguing that I was being unreasonable. Finally, at 4:00 a.m., I told him I was going to bed and that I had no intention of seeing him again.

When I woke up that morning, he had written back one last time to get the last word and then unfriended me. Good riddance.

I apologized to my brother the next morning. He told me that after I told him about seeing Luke, he had a really bad feeling that he couldn't shake and immediately started pacing his room, praying constantly for my safety. Finally, after praying for the Lord to send angels to protect me, he finally had peace and went to sleep just after midnight.

I was startled by that and told him what I had seen. At that, we both realized God had sent an angel on a bicycle that looked like my brother to help get me back to safety.

*You won't feel like an inconvenience.*

I was dating a guy long distance for a few months. While I lived as a flight attendant in southern Oregon, he lived in Salem, Oregon, which was three and a half hours away. Mutual friends from his church had set us up.

This was also the man who had admitted to me after a month or so that he had struggled with feeling like he was gay for as long as he could remember. But he wanted the nuclear family, and his mom wanted grandchildren from him. And as a Christian, he knew it was wrong, so he had been attending Celebrate Recovery for the last couple years, where he found peace and acceptance by those also struggling with various things.

So much of our relationship made sense after the fact. I always felt like he wasn't attracted to me, so I would try to be cuter and wore more skirts and dresses, but it never quite worked. And I found it strange when he made comments at times that he was surprised he was dating someone so feminine, as he always thought he would end up with someone more masculine. In hindsight, his random remarks made perfect sense. But at the time, it was confusing and consternating. The beginning of the end was when he went on a month-long hunting trip, which he took yearly. When he returned, I called him and explained how over the last month I had felt like an accessory or an afterthought. I felt like an inconvenience, a duty, an obligation. I knew he felt like hunting trips were a hiatus from life, but it was also a hiatus from me.

To go from talking or texting every day to barely acknowledging each other's existence was shell shock to my system. I reminded him how after his first week away, I told him how hard that had been for me. His response had been that I would simply need more "maintenance" in the following week. I explained that no one wants to hear that they require maintenance.

He had told me on multiple occasions that he found girls boring—but that I was the exception. Still, girls were boring, and for some reason I wasn't. The pressure mounted to not become a bore to him. And that pressure materialized into fear in the middle of his hunting trip when he told me for the second time that our phone conversations were boring. I felt like I wasn't enough—not interesting enough and not entertaining enough to be worth his time.

Considering that ours was a long-distance relationship, I didn't know how we could go on if we couldn't even talk on the phone. This was a conundrum to me because my top love language has always been quality time. And through talking on the phone, I was able to communicate and confide in people, which in turn made me feel loved.

I felt like he didn't need me and didn't want me, so I decided to try not to be selfish in wanting to text or talk to him in the last weeks of his hunting trip. But in that time of trying to stay away and give him man time, I was feeling left behind.

And in that space of feeling alone, I did what I loved and craved most—I praised and worshipped the Lord. I cried out to God and let Him penetrate through the cracks that had formed in my heart. As I let Him in, His healing salve seeped deep into my soul. And I started to feel that heavenly happiness that only happens with extended times of worship and communion with Him. All of a sudden, I found that my spiritual love tank was full, and I was overflowing with joy, peace, and contented bliss.

In contrast, even with my spiritual revelations of joy, my soul was still saddened by my hunting man's absence. When I tried to probe to see if Mr. Hunting Man missed me, he explained that he was just in his elk-box. So no, he didn't miss me, and he never once asked me what I was up to. That was the only answer I needed.

By the time I finished telling him everything that concerned me, he grew extremely angry. I was shocked to see that side of him. He was obviously done. And at that point, I was too.

It took me a good week of prayer and talking with my pastor to stop feeling verbally assaulted by the things he had said. But the Lord is faithful. And He allowed me to again bask in His presence and love, which overcame the hurt I had felt. If you get anything from this at all, I hope you can see how turning to the Lord with your pain is the only cure that satisfies and truly heals.

In regard to the gentleman, he had a cat, as I did. My cat was notorious for behavior problems, such as wetting my comforter if I didn't continue petting her when she wanted it. When I told that to Mr. Hunting Man, my then boyfriend, he was (rightfully) disgusted and insisted that his cat had never soiled anything.

After we had broken up, I asked Mr. Hunting Man to return my riding coat, which I had inadvertently left in his truck. Since I was living in southern Oregon, while he lived just a minute from my parents in Salem, it seemed like a simple solution that he could return it to them. So when he brought it over, my dad answered the door. My ex thrust my coat into his hands, mumbling that "the cat must have peed on it." And then he abruptly left. My dad informed me that it was definitely peed on. But it wasn't the typical rancid scent of cat urine. And that's when I recalled that his cat had never soiled anything before.

*God may let him know first.*

I was always the one to break up with a guy. I was the heartbreaker as soon as I found a deal breaker. And as such, breaking ties tended to be easier for me. As soon as I found a reason to say goodbye, my heart could often find the off switch and turn off the emotion for that person. Now, I understand I may be an anomaly in this. But I think it's because I wouldn't allow my heart to get truly involved until I had my questions answered satisfactorily. And if they weren't, I would say so long!

But that trend changed one day, and I truly didn't see it coming—even though my dad made it clear he didn't feel this was the man for me. I was blinded by surface emotion and excitement about this cowboy artist from Montana. He was different from anyone I had dated before. He was well mannered and kindhearted. He was a believer. And I was able to adjust my work schedule so that I could fly into his town for a twenty-four hour layover at least once a week for a couple months.

I tell this story to show how God works everything out to His will. And also, when a guy ends things with you because he discovered first that you aren't suited for each other, listen to him. And then don't pine after a relationship that wasn't meant to be. But take your heart before the Lord.

I thought things were going well. He took me to his church one Sunday and introduced me to his pastor. He showed me his art studio where he had crafted amazing paintings full of rustic charm and wildlife from nature photographs of horses, moose, buffalo, you name it.

Things were going so well with us that he flew into Oregon to meet my family over a holiday. And right after that, I flew down to Mexico on a mission trip. A few days later, I received an email. My amazing cowboy artist boyfriend was breaking up with me in an email. I felt like I had been pummeled in the gut. How couldn't I have seen that coming? Was that how the guys felt when I broke up with them?

He explained in the surprisingly thoughtful email that he had experienced a gnawing feeling ever since visiting my family and couldn't ignore it. He said it was very obvious that my family loved me very much and that I would never be happy in Montana. And he would never leave because that was where he got his inspiration for painting. That was where he belonged.

He also said that he had a very strong feeling that one day I would end up back in Salem. I got frustrated at that. Little did I know, the Lord had put it on his heart because several years later, I moved back to my hometown to marry my brother's best friend.

So it's important to remember that just because we want our life to go a certain direction, that's not always the way it will go. And the Lord can just as easily tell the person we are dating if He has different plans for our lives. He was telling me the same thing, but I wasn't listening. I wanted a life that wasn't for me. And in retrospect, living in Montana would have been boring for me, as I would have missed having my family and friends nearby.

I realized I still had more to say before we parted ways because I needed final closure, so we met up at a local diner. Mutual respect, admiration, and care for each other filled our last words. When he hugged me farewell, it reminded me of our first goodbye. This time, though, his last hug lingered. I almost cried as his fingers found my hair and gently stroked through a final time. This was I care about you. This was I'll miss you. This was goodbye. And closure. Sorrow had never felt so sweet, nor had sweetness felt so sorrowful.

The Lord used that relationship because it caused me to consider applying for the sister airline to the regional I was flying for. So just a week after he had broken up with me, I sent out my application and told the Lord that if it was His will, He would make it happen. I was prepared for a denial because becoming a flight attendant is very competitive. And even though I was flying for the sister company, it was certainly not a guarantee I would be accepted. But just two months later, I was offered the position, and within less than a year, I was not only working in my exciting new job, but living just an hour away from my family and had begun dating my now husband.

## My Waiting Takeaway

From these three dating experiences, I learned several valuable lessons.

### Mr. Facebook experience.

Spiritually, I realized that God cares and listens to our prayers and answers them, even in unconventional ways that we may not expect. If we ask for the Lord's will for our lives, and then if we find ourselves in the wrong relationship, He will always give us a way out. We just have to take it.

Physically, I recognized how dangerous situations can become. I learned that I need to not treat red flags flippantly. Oftentimes, red flags are our conscience discerning something that isn't right. Red flags can also simply be a feeling of warning from the Holy Spirit trying to save you from a bad situation.

Emotionally, it's also important to have solid friends before, during, and after romantic relationships. Just as you analyze your date's friends, he will be making observations about your friends too. You can learn a lot about a person by the people they spend the most time with. You naturally begin to emulate those who you are around. And that's why you want to surround yourself with God-loving friends who care about the Lord and who care about you.

Since then, I also realized that God very much cares about who we spend our time with, regardless of whether it's a dating relationship or a friendship. He wants us to have people in our lives who will encourage us, sharpen us, and be a good influence on us. And we should want to be those things for our friends too.

*Mr. Hunting Man experience.*

Most of the lessons I got from this experience were emotional and mental ones. First, a relationship isn't a relationship if it's one-sided. It never felt like a sacrifice for me to rearrange my work schedule to try to see him, yet he always acted as if it was such an inconvenience to make time for a date.

Second, when dating someone, you should *want* to see them every day. If you get married, then you *have to* see them every day.

Third, you shouldn't marry someone you can just live with. But you should only marry someone if you can't live without them. I definitely didn't get the impression that he couldn't live without me. It felt like he was more than happy without me. And no one wants to just be an accessory in another person's life. The bottom line is that I realized you need to feel like you're important to the man you're dating. If you don't feel like a priority while dating him, it will only get worse if you marry him. So I wanted to find someone who would make me feel cherished and beloved.

Fourth, I grappled with not feeling pretty enough through this entire relationship. It made sense in this context after I discovered his struggle with feeling gay. But my feelings highlighted an emotional battle that I and many women have faced: We struggle with equating outer beauty with our worth. The Lord has continually had to remind me that my worth is inherent in the fact that I am His; and it is my worth in Him that makes me beautiful. It's not the other way around.

*Mr. Montana experience.*

Emotionally, I learned that closure is important. At the time, though, it was difficult to come to terms with the breakup since something inside of me still wanted closure because it was over so quickly. And I realized that caring about someone didn't make them the right one for you, and it was just tough to accept.

Spiritually, I realized that even things that seem like denials are simply God's way of saying He has something better for you on the way. And that may be a year from now or ten years from now. We just have to wait patiently for His timing. That's one big trap we females can fall into: staying in the wrong relationship because we appreciate the attention and adoration. We may not even have feelings for the guy but choose to stay with him because we crave his praises. Sometimes he may not even be praising us; we simply want the male attention.

I learned that if we put our heart and trust in Him (our emotions and our spiritual future) He will always provide a physical way out of a wrong relationship. That may be through divine intervention as he sends angelic help your way. Or it may be Him highlighting how a man isn't treating you as he ought. Or God may tell the gentleman first that you are not a match. Regardless of the method, I learned that the Lord would always give me a way out of a relationship that wasn't His will for me.

## Your Waiting Step

God always provided me a way out of wrong relationships, and I'm confident He will do the same for you. Here are some tips that I hope you can take away from my experiences that will help you avoid staying with the wrong man.

Spiritually, are you taking time to keep your relationship with Christ first? By doing this, your spiritual senses will be sharpened to be keenly aware of warning signs in relationships. The Lord has given us the gift of the Holy Spirit to help gently guide us to the path of righteousness.

Emotionally, regularly keep track of how he makes you feel. Do you feel valued and cherished? Does he rearrange his schedule to see you? Does he make room for you in his life, or just try to fit you in? Does he make you feel like an inconvenience? These are all things to be aware of. Also, have you struggled with not feeling beautiful enough? This is something to take to God in prayer and ask Him to reveal how He sees you! Once you are reminded of how beautiful you are to Him, you will start to walk in that confidence.

Physically, God can give you a way out of a wrong relationship. It is up to you to take that out and leave the relationship. So watch for those. Is the man you're dating telling you he feels you aren't right for each other? Is he treating you in ways that are repeatedly not respectful or kind, which are reasons to bow out. Or is the Lord providing you what can only be described as a divine escape?

He can give you a plethora of warning signs, but it's up to you to respond to them.

Think about any past relationships. Were there signs that God was giving you that it wasn't meant to be? Did you listen to His warnings? Think about the ways I mentioned that can help you be attentive to His leading in the future. If you learn to recognize warning signs, it's easier to be cognizant in new relationships. And in some cases, you can end a wrong relationship before it begins.

## Your Waiting Journal Tips

If you've been in previous relationships, here are a few journal prompts.

1. Write down some of the things you've learned through them. How have those prepared you for a future relationship?
2. Did the Lord give you an amazing escape out of a wrong relationship? If so, write the story down, because you may be able to someday share it with someone else needing to make a great escape.
3. What are the red flags you experienced that you are now on the lookout for?

Here are a few more journal ideas that can also be for anyone who hasn't had previous relationships. The greatest way to have discernment in dating is through your spiritual senses. And the way to grow spiritually is to make your relationship with the Lord your priority.

1. What are some practical ways you can grow in your walk with Jesus? Can you designate time for prayer, worship, the Word, or sermons consistently through the week? Consider

writing down a devotional plan that can help you make Him your priority.

2. Write about some ways you can stay emotionally healthy, because if you go into a relationship healthy, you'll be able to more easily notice if it is an unhealthy emotional environment. What are hobbies or activities you like to do that will enhance your emotional well-being?

3. What are physical things you can do to stay healthy? Can you make better eating habits or exercise more frequently? List some goals you'd like to make that will add to your physical health.

## Verse and Prayer

"The Lord will fight for you; you need only to be still." (Eph. 14:14 NIV)

*Lord, thank You* that You are a good Father! You will save me out of every bad situation or relationship I may find myself in. Please give me the discernment to know when to keep myself from certain situations that would cause me pain. Thank You that You always fight for me and my well-being. Help me to be still in Your presence and listen to Your leading. I put my trust in You. In Your precious name. Amen.

# THE DOWN AND DIRTY
# ABOUT DATING

When I see the way society treats relationships so flippantly, I wonder what happened to the way we used to date. Words like *commitment* have become synonymous with *imprisonment* and *captivity*. Commitment has almost lost the meaning of diligence, dedication, and constant effort to protect something precious.

Even the concept of *relationship* has become too much of an emotional entanglement. So we simply say "dating" to keep our options open. Calling someone a "boyfriend" is just too confining. We don't want to be closed minded by limiting ourselves. Someone better might be just around the corner. Our happiness is dependent on our openness, right? No, but our selfishness is.

Even when we get in a "committed" relationship, we keep our eyes wide open. One eye on the present guy and the other eye on future prospects. And we can't forget past relationships because some men become more handsome in hindsight.

I remember thinking that the world was crazy when it introduced online dating. How many options does a person need? But the thing is, we can have all the smiles, winks, and flirts in the world, and it wouldn't be enough. Flirting has become a game. Even if you're not interested, the chime on your phone lets you know someone else is. So we play the game, wanting to feel wanted. We crave the compliments. The clever banter. The cat-and-mouse complex. It's as if our self-confidence depends on it.

Why can't we be confident without it? Why aren't one special someone's words of endearment and encouragement enough?

The deeper issue here is that instead of being thankful for what we have, we covet what we lack. We combine the attributes of past boyfriends—*his* personality with *his* humor and *his* abs—to create the perfect man. But once we come to the conclusion that the ideal doesn't exist, we comfort ourselves by craving—not the ideal—but the *next*. The next obsession. The next fix. The next confusing emotional mess that we ditch the second it gets too difficult.

With our expectations of needing to be entertained, anything that doesn't seem thrilling must in contrast be considered boring. But I want the mundane to be just as riveting as something exciting. To experience this begins with me internally.

Someone once said happiness is an inside job. It is. So is contentment and commitment in a relationship because it starts in the heart before we meet a prospective mate. If we aren't satisfied with ourselves, how can we be satisfied with someone else?

Why do we freak out if someone says they love us too soon? We want flirtatious falsities from strangers and then freak out when we find someone actually cares. Are we so afraid to love ourselves that we can't fathom how someone else could?

We shouldn't crave half-baked compliments from insincere men who only want what they can get. We don't want a relationship, love, and commitment because our world is becoming fast-food everything. But that's the thing—we know it's killing us, but we just keep eating and eating, feeding our obesity.

# Chapter 9

## ONLINE DATING

Let's think of online dating like fishing. It's possible to throw your net out and catch a lot of fish. And let's say you caught five interested fish in your net. You may feel a sense of security in having so many options. But if you have five fish in your bucket, they will all start looking the same—because you really don't *know* any of them.

Instead, place your energy into getting to know the one fish/dating profile that stands out among the rest. If you focus on one at a time, you'll more quickly determine if that one is worth your time and energy.

I've heard many love stories from married couples who met online. So I know it has a place and has been successful for some people. I was tired of being single, so my friend and I decided to make profiles on a popular Christian dating site. It seemed like a harmless idea, although I definitely entertained the worry that I might meet a serial killer from time to time. That being said, my experiences with online dating were a bit more complicated and frustrating and quite a mix. One guy I met cared too much and another not enough. Though I didn't meet my future husband online, I hope that by sharing my experiences with online dating, I can share some warnings of what to look out for, what I learned, and also a few tips along the way.

## My Waiting Story

In the next few stories, I will share my experiences of learning what chemistry wasn't, how someone can lie online, and also how important punctuality was to me (which you'll only learn if you meet face to face).

### Lacking chemistry and trust.

My first boyfriend was kind and caring—a country gentleman. I remember the day we met face to face at an ice cream shop; my best friend had told me to text her how it was going so she'd know if she should come save me from a dangerous or disastrous date. It turned out to be neither.

Since I'd never been in an actual boyfriend-girlfriend relationship up to that point, I was understandably swayed by excitement. So much so that I missed the signs that indicated we lacked chemistry. We were quite different individuals with differing interests. I first thought I could expand my interests and learn to like ranch life, horses, and the country in general. I liked it because it was vastly different from how I grew up living in the city. But there is a difference between enjoyment in gaining knowledge about something new and excitement of wanting to make it your lifestyle. He was good looking and kind, so I thought that was enough as far as chemistry went. I assumed that how I felt was how you were supposed to feel—I didn't know any differently.

Even after he kissed me for the first time, five months into dating, I rationalized my lack of intensity to assuming I was just one of the few who didn't like to kiss. (I really don't think anyone dislikes kissing when you're with someone you have chemistry with.)

It wasn't until I discovered some things he had been dishonest about that I began to question our relationship. Porn, alcoholism, and lying about both were major issues for me. Since honesty was high on my priority list of nonnegotiable attributes, I was devastated. Even though we lacked the chemistry needed for a long-term relationship, I still had let my heart think I was going to marry him. This was before I learned to put a protective shield about my heart when I started dating. That experience helped me recognize the importance of guarding my heart.

### Lacking honesty and chivalry.

The second guy I started getting to know online was both a firefighter and professional photographer. He seemed sweet, but was also what one might call *clingy*. We hadn't even met yet and he would message me constantly. Admittedly, I didn't mind at first. I was too distracted by the excitement that someone was infatuated with me to notice.

We would Skype before FaceTime was even a thing. The quality wasn't terribly good, though. In retrospect, it was probably due to his dimly lit house. I was impressed by his talent on the guitar, which he played for me whenever we ran out of words. He also played at his church, which earned him brownie points in my book.

Two months into our online relationship, he decided to come up to meet me, along with my family, for Thanksgiving. It seemed like a good idea. From the moment he stepped out of his car, I realized several things simultaneously. First, he was actually pretty much the same height as me, which gave me pause since his profile had indicated that he was several inches taller than me. The height wouldn't have been a problem to me if he had been honest about it online. Second, I immediately noticed the smell. It seemed a stench emanated from his body, though I gave him the benefit of the doubt that perhaps it was the eight-hour drive from California. Third, I noticed acne covered his entire face—acne that was oddly missing in all of his photos. Since he was a professional photographer, I surmised he had doctored his photos.

I wanted someone who would be up front with me from the get-go, because that's when you're starting to form trust with the person. As you can probably imagine, he already had three strikes against him.

After that initial day of introductions, my parents allowed him to stay the night in their RV. The next day, he took me rock climbing. The activity was fun, but his BO remained. I rationalized that perhaps it was from the vigorous workout he'd had rock climbing. We didn't have much meaningful conversation that day since we went from rock climbing to hiking.

Another thing I noticed was everywhere we went that cost something—from meals to the indoor rock climbing—he never once offered to pay. So I paid for us both.

The next day was Thanksgiving, so he met my entire extended family. He acted a bit awkward around everyone. I reasoned it was nerves, but soon I realized he had been acting oddly since he arrived. I didn't find his humor funny, and I was embarrassed when he cracked up at his own jokes when no one else did. After Thanksgiving, I realized that the body odor wasn't due to the drive or the hike or the rock climbing but must have been poor hygiene.

I knew I had to end things. The next day, we went to breakfast, where I proceeded to explain that I didn't think we were a good match. He was completely shocked. It took two hours of trying to convince him that I was serious—all the while he cried off and on. I felt so bad for him, but I wasn't attracted to him in the way that was necessary for a romantic relationship.

*Lacking punctuality.*

The next guy I met online cared too little. He seemed like a perfect catch because my cousin knew him from high school. We'll call him Johnny. Our first date was that he would pick me up to go out to lunch. I remember sitting on the couch at the designated time he would arrive. I shifted nervously as the clock kept ticking. After twenty minutes, I decided to refresh my makeup.

After thirty minutes, I texted him and innocently asked if I had gotten the day wrong. He said no, but that he was out to coffee with friends and had lost track of time; but he assured me he was on his way and said where he was coming from. I knew the street was about ten minutes away without traffic. So I watched the clock. A half an hour later, he arrived.

I tried not to show my disappointment, even though I had always thought first dates were important for making good first impressions. Still, I decided to reserve judgement until after we ate.

As we dug into our meals, I quickly forgot about his tardiness. He was very social, amiable, and friendly. Considering how easily he could hold his own end of a conversation, it was no wonder he was late. I thought he must have treated every conversation with equal importance, which is why one social event caused him to be late to the next. It made rational sense in my brain at the time.

By the next week, we had a second date planned. Unfortunately, the day before, he said his dad was in town (who was a truck driver who worked for my ex-boyfriend's family's trucking business). He said he wanted to see his dad instead. I tried not to be hurt. Family was important. I didn't know how long his dad had been gone, but it still stung a little that he couldn't carve out even an hour from his reunion to have a little date he had already committed to. We rescheduled for another week out. He seemed like a decent, hardworking, Christian man, so I would gave him the benefit of the doubt.

It was finally our second face-to-face date. He was taking me out to dinner. I knew it was a nice local restaurant, so I wore a fancy dress and heels for the occasion. Again, I sat anxiously on the couch. Minutes passed. I started getting a sinking feeling as I remembered what had happened the last time.

He was supposed to arrive at 5:30. I intentionally hadn't eaten much for lunch so I would be hungry at our dinner date. Pretty soon, it was six. So, with a wave of de ja vu, I texted him again asking if he was picking me up or if we were meeting at the restaurant.

He responded a few minutes later that he was picking me up. I breathed a sigh of relief that I had the correct day and it didn't seem as if he had forgotten. I hoped.

As the minutes crawled into slow motion, my stomach started growling angrily, and my heart started sinking. I was raised to believe that ten minutes early was on time, while on time was late. And if you cared about someone, you would respect their time because time was a commodity. When he finally arrived just as the clock struck seven (an hour and a half late), I stopped hoping he might be a candidate for my heart.

Admittedly, I enjoyed our dinner—probably because I was famished and he was just so incredibly social and easy to get along with. When he asked to set up another date next week, I agreed. Just days later, he asked to reschedule. At that point, I put all the pieces together and decided I didn't want to put my heart through a roller coaster relationship with a guy who wasn't fully invested. So I ended things with him. He too acted shocked. I guessed that he didn't get rejected often because of his charming personality.

## My Waiting Takeaway

The biggest conclusion I made while online dating was: You really can't know a person if your relationship is strictly online. In every instance, I didn't discover deal breakers until I met each guy face to face. And I learned lessons through each experience.

*First boyfriend.*

I learned that I was in love with the idea of love. But I wasn't in love with him. That's a dangerous place to be because feelings fade. Whereas true love will stand with you through it all. True love may start as a feeling, but then it becomes a choice to love someone every day and every minute of the day.

I also concluded that chemistry was just as important as finding someone who shared my faith. Just because we had the same theological standpoints didn't mean we were a good romantic match. And I also realized how important trust is in a relationship. If someone lies about even seemingly insignificant things, you will start to wonder how you can trust them with larger things . . . not the least of which being your heart.

I also learned the importance of guarding my heart. Proverbs 4:23 (NLT) says, "Guard your heart above all else, for it determines the course of your life." Falling for someone is a wonderful feeling, but make sure the man you are falling for is worth your heart. If not, the ending will only provoke more heartache than you would have had otherwise. The times I guarded my heart in relationships were the times that I was able to let go easily. When I would end a dating relationship, it was like an instant off switch.

*Photo-doctoring firefighter.*

My first takeaway from meeting this firefighter in person was that looks can be deceiving online. You can't see through the computer screen to know what they smell like and how they act. You really have to meet in person to get that information.

After having to pay for both him and me on all the outings, I realized that a girl wants to know that the man will *want* to provide for her physically, monetarily, and spiritually in their relationship; so if he won't offer to even pay for himself, it's natural to start to doubt that he will want to take care of her and their future children in a marriage relationship. Even though it's perfectly acceptable for a woman to contribute to a relationship monetarily, it is in a man's DNA to want to provide. God wired them that way. So if a guy doesn't show the desire to provide, you may end up taking care of his and your children's needs if you marry him. That was certainly a red flag for me.

*Mr. Unpunctual.*

First, I realized I cared more about feeling appreciated than about being with a great catch. I realized that lack of punctuality can equate a lack of interest—at least, that's how it makes the recipient feel.

Second, I found that I'm more like my family than I realized in that I want to value people's time, and I want others to value mine.

Third, this was the relationship where I learned about the "breakup sandwich," which worked well in this instance. You start by telling them something you like about them, and in the middle, put the jelly of why it won't work out, and then end it with building them up again. In my experiences, I found that this approach really did help lessen the blow. The guy tended to take the news better if it was softened.

As I mentioned earlier in the book, some guys are only interested in flirting or a fling. I had to exercise discernment to sift through to discern between who was after my body and who was after my heart.

**Your Waiting Step**

If you go the online dating route, tread carefully. Go in with both eyes wide open. Pray diligently before meeting someone face to face. Here are some red flag warnings to be aware of when dating.

*Red Flag #1 to Watch For*

**Pay attention to if he is honest with you.** If you guard your heart, you will be open to noticing any dishonesty as opposed to ignoring things you don't like. Guarding your heart is not to say you shouldn't put yourself out there in a relationship. My philosophy was always: put it all on the table, tell him who you are and what you believe, and then it's his turn to decide to be equally forthcoming with you.

*Red Flag #2 to Watch For*

**Does he start to care too much too soon?** If so, he will allow his heart to get so entangled that after first meeting, he will have a harder time accepting that you don't want to continue a relationship.

*Red Flag #3 to Watch For*

**Discern whether this is someone who only wants to flirt.** Most importantly, listen to the still, small whisper of the Holy Spirit when He lets you know someone is not the one for you.

Along with red flags to watch for, there are some cautions to consider. Cautions aren't necessarily red flags and should be evaluated with the possibility of them turning out okay.

*Caution #1 to Consider: Confusing the Details*

A side effect of online dating was that it became obvious that I was not the only girl they were dating because a guy would get me confused with another girl. They would insist that I said or did something in the past that I hadn't. And oftentimes, they were things that I wouldn't ever do, which made it even more obvious that the girl they were referring to was not me. That made me a little uncomfortable because I approached online dating just how I would approach regular dating—one bachelor at a time. Like I mentioned at the beginning of the chapter, I didn't want my fishing rod in different ponds. How are you supposed to analyze the intricacies of the fish you caught if it's not the only one?

*Caution #2 to Consider: In a Hurry*

Another large takeaway I had from online dating was that the men I met on Christian dating sites were so desperate to get married they didn't make certain I was the one they wanted to marry. It was as if I fit the preliminary description of someone they wanted to marry, so they didn't need to know anything more. However, I was not ready to jump into marriage that quickly! Remember to get that list of questions answered, and take the time needed to see if their character is as good in person as it may seem on paper. It's an exciting, nerve-wracking place to be getting to know someone new. You can be open and vulnerable with telling someone who you are and then wait to see how he'll respond.

Here's the exciting thing. We get to practice being raw and open and vulnerable by opening our hearts up to Jesus first. Because, as I've mentioned before, we need to find our inner peace through our relationship with Him first, and only then will we find peace in the right relationship. How do we find inner peace in Christ? Peace comes from surrender. When we surrender our desires and ask the Lord to replace them with His desires, He honors our sacrifice. And He will honor our request because He wants us to choose His path for our lives. Choosing to lay down our own hopes will result in the sweetness of peace. I have had to lay down my own will so many times. And every time, He honors that surrender with an all-encompassing peace and assurance that He will take care of me.

The center of His will is where we want to strive to be. Let's not hang on to the fringes of His will, dancing the line. We should want to be so enclosed in the center of His will that we don't have to worry about having a slight deviation pull us off of His path.

Sometimes we mistake our feelings for His will. And that's why keeping a close relationship with the Lord is imperative. The more time we spend getting close to Him, the more certain we will be of His Holy Spirit's nudges.

## Your Waiting Journal Tips

Write a list of characteristics or habits that you *don't* want in a husband. These are now going to be your red flags if you see them exhibited in a date. If you're considering if the online dating route is right for you, I would first ask you to pray and ask the Lord to direct you.

Let's go back to the first lists you wrote of what you *do* want in a husband. When you see a profile that catches your interest, weigh the things he says about himself with these lists. If he passes the red flag test and you've considered the cautions, pray about that person—and ask the Lord for His heart on the matter.

## Verse and Prayer

"Guard your heart above all else, for it determines the course of your life." (Prov. 4:23 NLT)

*Lord Jesus, thank You* so much that You always have my best interests in mind, even when I can't see the full picture. I pray that You will increase my gift of discernment. Help me see through the frauds and fakes who may try to take my heart. I ask that I will grow so close in my relationship with You that I will be able to know right away if a relationship is worth pursuing or not. And I pray that the man I am to marry someday will be able to grow close to

You in this time that we're apart. Give him wisdom and discernment as well so that he doesn't have to go through unnecessary heartache before we are united. I surrender my heart and desires into Your loving, capable hands. In Jesus's name. Amen.

# ROSES AND THORNS

Within a week, he pulled me in like a whirlwind,
or like the fragrant scent of a rose bush
beckoning me with its beauty
to lean in and breathe in.
But I didn't see the thistles
that lined each stem
until they penetrated my skin,
severing veins and tendons,
paralyzing me into reliving that week on repeat—
How could something that smelled so sweet
be so sharp and splintering?
Even so, is it silly that I miss the sound of his voice?
Scruff on his face?
And the grasp of his hand?
I even miss the clanking of change
inside his pants pocket.
He opened my eyes to a new way of looking at things,
things I wouldn't have otherwise seen,
a different, sadder side to the world
that I didn't know existed.
Yet I can only offer sympathy.

As much as I want to empathize,
I can't relate
to growing up with violence and hate.
And as I sit here pondering the cruelty of life
and the unfair hand life deals,
I can't help but feel
unjustified
in my pain of missing him,
considering it's nothing
compared to all that he's been through.

# Chapter 10

## WHEN YOU KNOW YOU'RE ATTRACTED TO THE WRONG GUY

Dating is like an audition. The part is the role of costar in the story of your life. If each date is an audition, you're the casting director deciding if the candidate is worthy of a callback. Sometimes we give callbacks to guys who may not have given a stellar performance, but we see potential, so we give them another chance to prove that the last audition was a fluke. If it wasn't, that's when we kindly tell them that they just aren't quite suited to the role but that we're certain they will find a role that fits them perfectly.

Unfortunately, we sometimes give guys callbacks who continually give poor performances or who we know aren't meant to be our costar. Why? It's called infatuation, and it's a part of the human condition. The good news is that you are stronger than you think and can say so long to the no-goes.

Have you ever been attracted to someone who was totally wrong for you and you knew it? It's happened to me more than once, and every date ended in breakup.

When you are attracted to someone and you discover they are attracted to you, it can be an almost magical feeling. Psychologically we tell ourselves that mutual attraction must mean something and is some sort of sign. But it's not. Attraction in and of itself is a fact of life.

You may even find yourself attracted to someone for all the wrong reasons. For me, the wrong reasons had been wealth, a sense of humor, and the redeemed bad boy. None of those reasons in and of themselves should warrant having a relationship with someone.

## My Waiting Story

I had two dating experiences with wealthy men and one dating experience with a homeless man. I found something attractive about each of them, but that didn't make any of them right for me.

### Family fortune over kindheartedness.

The first wealthy man I dated treated me like a second-class citizen. And I was so twitterpated and oblivious to see it until my friends met him and pointed it out. After that, I couldn't stop seeing how degrading his attitude was toward me. He came from a family of wealth with a grandfather worth billions, while my family owned a small business. Mr. Wealthy acted like you couldn't even compare one with the other.

He was also an alcoholic who bragged about getting snookered on his guys' weekend escapades. In retrospect, that was so not attractive. At the time, I was a naive twenty-three-year-old who was just excited to have the attention of someone more worldly wise and wealthy (and a Christian). It wasn't until I was about twenty-six that I started realizing how naive I was in the world of men and dating.

Through that experience, I soon learned not to be swooned by wealth. It's better to be with someone who makes a little and treats you like a priceless gem than someone who gives you diamonds but treats you like garbage.

*Scientifically brilliant but socially lacking.*

The next man I dated for the wrong reasons was a well-to-do nuclear engineer. He was actually my fourth attempt at online dating after thinking I was done with the outlet. That relationship was long distance, since he lived in Bremerton, Washington, and I was still a flight attendant in southern Oregon.

He certainly fit the mold for his career. Quiet, shy, and socially awkward. We wrote each other letters, and he was so articulate with pages and pages of deep, thought-provoking material. As someone with a degree in English, I was enamored of who he portrayed himself to be on paper. But on our first date (at a sandwich shop), he was too shy to order for himself and whispered the items he wanted on his sandwich so I could relay them back to the attendant. It was almost embarrassing.

But he had a good job and was so articulate on paper that I really wanted it to work. During our painfully awkward lunch, there were several times I could see that he had something he wanted to say but just couldn't get the right words out. I felt for him and so very much wanted to hand him a piece of paper and say, "Please, just write down what you're trying to say." But I didn't want to come across as rude. So I sat there watching him stumble through, his mouth gaping open, with grunts and "ah" sounds.

As frustrating as our lunch had been, I convinced myself that he just had a bad case of first-date jitters. After I flew home, I found a beautifully written letter explaining what a wonderful time he'd had. So I decided to continue our letters, and a month later, I gave him another shot at a date.

This time he took me to the Space Needle. It was a kind gesture even though he made a stink about how expensive it was. Apparently, even though he made plenty of money and had a nice house, he still was upset over money. He even mentioned that he kept his house temperature below sixty degrees to save money. I was shocked. As someone who gets cold easily, I could very well picture myself having to dress in layers, with fleece mittens and blankets if I ended up with him.

But just like our previous date, as soon as we had to interact with each other, the awkwardness commenced. I wondered if he ever had an easy conversation with anyone.

He had given me a book by one of my favorite authors, which was such a thoughtful gesture that I decided to give him a third date. But then he also gave me a heart-shaped necklace with an inscription: J & B forever. He also intimated that he wanted to marry me. I was first swayed by the gifts and thoughtfulness, but then later I thought, *Hold the phone! I have only been writing you a couple months. I have no intention of marrying you yet!*

Additionally, his incessant halitosis was hard to ignore. I started offering him breath mints because it didn't only smell while he was talking, but just his normal inhale-exhale had a wretched stench. Since his teeth were quite yellow, I surmised he rarely brushed them.

Now, even after all these signs, I still flew him down to Salem to meet my family. And they wondered, as they had many times before, what on earth I was thinking. After that, I knew what I had to do.

He and I had scheduled another date, but I cancelled on him. I just couldn't go through with it. After I ended it, he called, bawling, and left an unintelligible message on my phone. I felt sorry for him along with a twinge of guilt for letting it go on even those couple months.

And then about a week later, I received an email from him.

It was a long spreadsheet he had created listing the names of all the women who had rejected him. My name was number 58. The columns had the duration of his pursuit, if the lady accepted him for who he was (no one apparently had), if she was a believer, if he had kissed her, and the reason for the breakup. I was shocked and slightly disturbed.

I wrote back that I didn't want my name on any such list. He mistook my meaning and responded that he didn't want my name on that list either: he wanted to marry me. I decided not to continue writing him to avoid giving him any more false hope. I am pleased to report that he did eventually get married, and I hope he is well and enjoying married life.

*Homeless, but such a sense of humor.*

The last guy (we'll call him Davy) I dated was literally a complete polar opposite of the man I would marry.

Davy was the bad boy who had found Christ after living a hard life. We met at church one Sunday night when I noticed him for the first time. I had seen him around church before, but actually sitting next to this rougher-looking man made my heart beat a little faster. After the service, he and I started chatting, and he walked me to my car. I quickly discovered there was nothing frightening about this scruffy-faced, shaggy-haired man who was just as saved by God's grace as I was. In fact, hearing him talk about the Lord suddenly made him attractive.

Yet this particular chap had an uncle who'd ridden with Hell's Angels until he ended up in prison. The chap had a horrible relationship with his "pops," who only provoked him to anger when he saw him, and he hadn't seen his mom since he was young. He said that she was undiagnosed but psychiatrically crazy and had done horrible things when he and his sister were children. He grew up in poverty, living on the wrong side of the tracks, with little to no supervision. He had no boundaries or rules. As you can imagine, he had some run-ins with the "Po-Po," as he called them, as early as age fifteen. That was what I knew of his childhood.

We started Facebook messaging each other, and then we started hanging out. He was kind and thoughtful and had a big heart. I soon discovered that because of the injustices he'd experienced growing up, he strongly detested injustice when he saw it. So he would stand up against it. But it could also sometimes get him worked up, I often noticed.

I soon realized that under that tough exterior was a walking paradox: Davy was a man with a tender heart and a boy with a broken spirit, and he was also a man who had anger toward the world for all its injustices. And he had his head full of both dreams and conspiracy theories that he could talk about for hours.

But it was his complexities that seemed to make him even more appealing. And that is partly why I ignored my deal breakers with him. I also ignored them because at that point, I had dated so many guys who turned out to be duds, I was over it. I thought perhaps there wasn't a perfect man for me. And perhaps I would just have to be content with the relationship I found myself in.

But I was ignoring quite a lot of my deal breakers. Davy was a cusser, a relapsing/recovering alcoholic, and a smoker, which he had been ever since he was a teenager. I also discovered after a while that he smoked marijuana too (before it was legal in Oregon). He insisted that it helped his ADD. He had been on it as "medicine" ever since the first grade when his dad introduced him to it. Even so, I saw how different he was when he was stoned, and it wasn't for the better, in my opinion. He was more self-centered and always insisted that I was interrupting him, which he considered a high form of disrespect.

That was actually one thing that bothered me the most. He got terribly upset if he perceived that I was trying to interrupt him. Often those "interruptions" would be me saying "ahh" or "I see" while he was relaying a story. I personally like it when someone indicates that they are paying attention to me when I'm talking, but he took offense to it.

I was aware that I didn't like how I was being treated, but I enjoyed my time with him so much that I didn't care. He had the best sense of humor and could make me laugh so hard my sides hurt. Up to that point, I hadn't dated anyone who could make me laugh like that. And I liked not being the funniest person in the relationship.

But having someone you get along with who can make you laugh doesn't mean you belong together. We didn't date for very long initially (maybe a week) but remained friends because we got along so well. And as you might have guessed, we started dating again a few months later. Being just friends with a guy you dated doesn't work very well. Even if you can somehow manage not to date again, think about how your future husband will feel if you tell him about your close guy friend whom you used to date. Do you think your husband will fully trust that neither of you will want to cross that bridge again if you're still in a close relationship with your ex?

Now, during the initial week of dating Davy, he told me that he had a bad habit of sleepwalking. During these episodes, he would do potentially dangerous things that he wouldn't remember, such as dropping a television on his foot or trying to start his car, though he couldn't get the key into the ignition.

I thought it was odd that he told me this, but I really didn't think it would be pertinent since he wouldn't be sleeping with me! But just a short time later, he fell asleep at my house while we were watching a movie. When the credits started rolling, I couldn't wake him. The house had gotten dark, so when he stood up, I didn't realize he was still asleep. He walked toward the front door. When I asked him if he was leaving, there was no response.

All of the sudden I heard a whooshing sound. I stood behind him, frozen at the couch. I realized he was *peeing*—yes, peeing—in my cat's water fountain. After what seemed like forever, the sound turned to a trickle and stopped. I breathed a sigh of relief. And as if nothing had happened, he came back and sat on the couch, still asleep.

I finally was able to shake him awake.

"Was I asleep?" he asked. "Oh no, what did I do?"

"You really don't remember?" I asked, somewhat flabbergasted.

After he insisted he didn't, I told him what had happened. He was mortified and embarrassed, and without lingering in his discomfort, he quickly left. So I cleaned up the mess, which had also soiled the rug under the cat bowl and the lower portion of the wall next to the front door.

In spite of having that hiccup early on, we remained friends.

When I learned that he was living out of his car and his source of income was doing odd jobs for people and janitorial work at the church, I felt sorry for his homelessness. I eventually let him house sit for me when I was out of town. It seemed like an intelligent arrangement, since I was away so much with my job.

But not terribly long into our agreement, my mom came down for a visit. I told her about my house sitter (even about the cat bowl), and she was far from pleased. She tried talking reason into me, but I didn't see it.

She then told me she couldn't keep things from my dad since they were very transparent with each other. I told her I understood. After church, she put dad on speaker phone as I drove. She only told him the bare minimum about my house sitter, excluding the cat bowl incident.

I should insert here that my dad hears the Lord, often quite clearly. And sometimes he says things that are from the Lord without even realizing it. After dad tried to talk me out of the arrangement and why it wasn't appropriate, he added, "You never know what he's going to pee on."

After a moment, I asked, "Why did you just say that?"

"I don't really know. It just felt like the thing to say."

At that point, I informed him that the peeing had already happened. And that one statement he'd made was more convincing to me than any of their well-articulated arguments. So while my mom was still in town, I asked Davy to return my spare key.

## My Waiting Takeaway

Reading this, you may be wondering why on earth I dated these guys in the first place. I share these stories to show you just how blind you can be when dating the wrong guys. They say love is blind. But I think true love sees everything and loves anyway.

Conversely, infatuation is blind. You're blinded by someone's true character when they're wooing you with whispered words, jewelry, or humor. And sometimes you see it and just ignore it.

Again, I learned specific things through each failed relationship.

### Wealth does not make the man.

The Bible warns about the dangers of wealth. Not only is it easier for a camel to go through the tiny eye of a needle than for a prosperous man to get into heaven (Matt. 19:24), Jesus also told a rich man, "If you want to be perfect, go, sell your possessions and give to the poor, and you will have treasure in heaven, Then come, follow me" (Matt. 19:21 NIV).

With the wealthy alcoholic who treated me like I was less important, I learned that wealth does not make a man. What makes a man is how he treats people. And since he didn't treat me like a treasure, I recognized that wealth was his treasure.

### Brilliant but too quick.

Just because I fit the profile of someone he wanted to marry, I realized that he decided far too quickly that he wanted me to be his wife. I learned that I really wanted a man who was interested in getting to know about my character, the facets of my personality, and especially about my faith before deciding he wanted to marry me.

I also realized that, as a social person myself, I valued being with someone who was also outgoing in social situations. Everyone is different, but for me, I realized that the outgoing quality would have to be moved from my *negotiable* list to my *nonnegotiable* one.

*Humorous but homeless.*

My biggest lesson here was that just because someone can make you laugh, it doesn't mean you belong together. Humor alone does not equate to happiness. I also learned that I wanted to date and marry someone who had a job and didn't enjoy living out of his car. It may seem like a simple desire, but at the time, it was a revelation to me.

## Your Waiting Step

I tell you my stories because I want to show that the sooner you break ties with someone who is not your future husband, the easier it will be and the less emotional baggage you will bring into your marriage someday. If you know a relationship isn't right, cut ties before you feel too tied in to escape. Trust me—you'll be happier in the long run.

When someone shows their true colors, show them the door. When someone doesn't treat you how a daughter of the Most High King should be treated, say goodbye. When you realize you're more swayed by gifts than by the person who gives them, don't accept any more. The sooner you realize that your feelings are infatuation, the sooner you can and should part ways because infatuation alone doesn't last.

It's true that some gals do marry bad boys turned Christians, but I have heard from some that the lives they lead together are more difficult with higher potential for problems. A man's past (of drug or alcohol abuse, women, porn addiction, or tendency toward violence) can potentially cause issues and consequences in the marriage, especially if he has not found true healing in Christ. And if he has properly dealt with his "stuff" and found healing in Christ, and if God calls you to that life, it's best to heed God's will because His plans for our lives are better than our plans. It may not be easy, but what it will produce in us will be good.

I want to stress that attraction in and of itself isn't wrong. I was and still am attracted to my husband. But when it's the wrong person, untethered attraction can lead to infatuation, and infatuation can lead you into a long detour of regret. If it's an unholy attraction, it cannot lead to love—although you'll try to convince yourself it is. I'll discuss more about that in the next chapter.

## Your Waiting Journal Tips

Have you given callbacks to auditions that were less than stellar? Did it turn out that the first audition was a fluke, or were they really unable to act in the play of your life? What did you learn from those experiences? Write down a prayer asking the Lord to allow you to quickly identify when you're attracted to someone who isn't right for you, and ask the Lord to do the same for your future husband.

## Verse and Prayer

"Promise me, O women of Jerusalem, by the swift gazelles and the deer of the wild, not to awaken love until the time is right." (Song of Solomon 2:7 NLT)

*Lord, please help* me to keep love from awakening prematurely when dating. I ask for You to highlight when I become attracted to the wrong person so that I can stop it from going any further. I don't want to have unnecessary burdens to work through in marriage. So I ask that You will grant me wisdom so that I do not fall into the trap of infatuation. Help me keep You front and center in this stage of my life. In Your name. Amen.

# THE FIX

No one warned me
that dating you was like doing drugs.
I was desperate for that daily dose,
whether snorted, shot, or smoked,
powder, needle, bong.
Schools taught me
to stay away from drugs.
So I took the dare
to defy the pressure of peers
and didn't do what others did.
But I didn't know you were like poison
seeping in my veins,
surging through my bloodstream,
like a foreign substance, unrecognized
but accepted without resistance
or hesitation.
Instead, my body bonded with the poison,
needing more to pacify
what couldn't be satisfied.
But each hit I took,
getting my fill, flirting with danger,

only intensified the addiction.
I finally saw what it was doing to me,
and knew who you were just wasn't like me,
and decided we needed to end.
But I made you feel like the villain.
And I didn't feel justified knowing you felt vilified.
Eventually, I explained it so you knew
I still cared for you,
and hadn't realized that
stopping your calls
would cause these heart-wrenching,
teeth-clenching, body-shaking withdrawals.
But that shouldn't have meant I'd return.
So I ended it again, but on good terms.
Sometimes I wonder if that's worse,
thinking I'm over getting stoned,
until your name shows on my phone.
And every stride I made dissipates
as my hands start to shake
and my heart becomes
intoxicated
and then exasperated
for falling so swiftly for something
I know I can't keep.
Does temptation ever leave?
Is recovery never-ending?
Or will I always struggle
with the self-inflicted scabs and scars
up and down my arms,
in and on my heart?
I hadn't known that dating you
would be the most addictive drug.

# Chapter 11

## DATING A NONBELIEVER

Imagine the person you're dating is a fruit. If you consume a fruit before it's ripe, it will be tart and unpalatable, and some fruits can actually cause more bodily harm than others. An unripe plum, for instance, will likely just give you an unfortunate stomachache. But if you consume unripe Lychees, found in India, the result can cause seizures and even death.

Now assuming you're dating an unripe plum, he may be a "nice guy" but not the one for you, and staying in this wrong relationship will likely give you a sour taste in your mouth and bad stomachache. But if he's an unripe Lychee (an unsaved man), staying in a relationship with him can have life-altering and life-threatening results. If you stay unequally yoked, you risk potential spiritual death.

**My Waiting Story**

Sometimes it seems like yesterday. Other times it seems like a lifetime ago. His name was William. Our story was by far the most emotionally painful of any that came before. But it's a story that needs to be told. I will be honest about my part in it, and I won't sugarcoat what happened. If sharing it will help just one person (perhaps you?) avoid the heartache I experienced, it will be worth it.

Even though I was well versed in the dating game, with William, everything was different. It was the first time I felt what I surmised was real chemistry—the butterflies, the heart-stopping fireworks, and what I thought was love.

But the problem was that William wasn't right for me, and I knew it. But I was sure that I would never feel the explosive excitement I had when around him with any other man. Yet that was just one of the lies I believed during that painful time.

I was a brand-new flight attendant. With the ability to simply hop on a plane and fly anywhere, I felt like the whole world was at my fingertips. My adventure-seeking, independent self didn't even consider once that danger or pain could be lurking around the next cloud.

With just over a month of flying under my belt, I was working a trip that took me on a route that went through Boise, Idaho. I was the flight attendant in the front of the plane, greeting everyone as they boarded. My big, silly smile was completely genuine as I welcomed everyone on board.

When he stepped on board, the Customer Service Agent (CSA) was giving him a hard time about something, but in a familiar way that denoted they were comrades. My heart did a little somersault when I saw how attractive he was. I was internally pleased when I saw that his assigned seat was in the front row, right across from my jump seat. The next thing I noticed was his soccer jersey, which had the name of my airline on it. So I asked, "Do you work for us?"

He grinned widely. "Yup. I work on the ramp here in Boise. I'm headed to Portland to catch the game!" He indicated to his jersey.

We immediately started making conversation.

During the drink service, I asked to see his ID when he asked for a microbrew. I studied his license photo a bit longer than was necessary. "You are my age!" I exclaimed. And that comment spurred on more small talk between us.

The flight attendant I was working with raised her eyebrows and grinned as she gazed from me to the guest in 1B and back to me again. As soon as we got to the back of the plane, she gushed, "Well, how's that for fireworks?"

"Was it that obvious?" I blushed.

She laughed heartily in response and handed me another complimentary beer to bring up to him. I didn't even care that I had issues with guys who drank. I didn't even care if he was an alcoholic. The rational part of my brain decided to stop functioning entirely.

By the end of the flight, the dashing fellow in 1B leaned over and handed me a folded piece of paper and said, "In case you find yourself in Boise again and want a tour guide." After he left, I opened up the paper—which turned out to be his boarding pass—and found his phone number handwritten across the top. I carried that boarding pass with me everywhere I went for a very long time.

On my next flight that day, I had a flight attendant onboard who said she was based in Boise. So I asked if she knew anything about the man I had just met named William. She did and went on about what a sweetheart he was. She said one of the older Boise agents had just lost her elderly mother, and he had brought her flowers. I was eating up every kind word she had to say about him.

So by that night, when I got to my hotel room, I couldn't keep my fingers from punching in his number and sending a quick text. He responded immediately. And thus it started.

When I started texting him about being a Christian, he responded that he grew up in a Christian home and that his mom had taught him about the Lord. He didn't mention having a personal relationship with God as I had, but I ignored that and chose to be encouraged by his belief in God. Wasn't that good enough?

*From flying high to meeting the ground fast.*

Within just weeks, he dropped the truth bomb. I discovered that he didn't share his mother's faith. So I ended things. I was heartbroken, but I was thankful that he was honest with me when he saw just how important my faith was to me.

Several days later, he texted me. It was a simple text that he missed me. That was all it took to get me texting again. I thought just texting was harmless. But texting was still talking, and talking to him created soul ties that continued to grow deeper the more we conversed.

Everything was all daisies, roses, and butterflies while we were talking, but the moment I put my phone down, I felt that gnawing again, that knowing feeling that it wasn't right. That inner voice repeated: *flee while you can.* I had to end the communication once more because I'd have no peace until I did.

But I'd rationalize. What's the harm in talking? What's the harm in texting? We live in separate states, for goodness' sake. And although we both had free standby flying privileges, my job made it difficult to see each other (which I see in hindsight was actually a blessing). But there was harm. Much harm.

*Listen to others and to God.*

Through the entire summer we had an on-and-off relationship; all the while I had good friends and family nudging me, sometimes prodding, with truth that I couldn't deny. Initially I told my friends I would not date him or become his girlfriend and certainly wouldn't marry him. I said this even though our relationship was based on romantic interest in each other.

I thought he was genuinely a great guy. Certainly by the world's standards, he was a rare gem. I'd probably correlate that to him being raised by a Christian mother. But his dad was not a believer. So to him, my concerns seemed unfounded because his parents were still happily married. Granted, I don't know their story or if his mother is like other Christian wives I know who go to church without their husbands, praying continually and desperately for their spouse's salvation.

My relationship with Christ affects every part of my life and is intertwined with what I do and who I am. No matter how *good* a man he was, that he didn't share my faith meant he couldn't share the most important part of my life. And that tore me apart inside.

One day, my best friend pointedly asked, "What kind of spiritual leader will he be if you marry a baby Christian?" That hit its mark because she'd heard me say over our many years of friendship that I broke things off with every Joe, Bill, and Bob because I didn't want a surface Christian, but I wanted a spiritual leader. Someone who didn't talk the talk but walked the walk—and someone who attended church Sunday not out of religious duty, but because he had a relationship with Jesus.

I wanted someone who could sharpen me in the Lord as I could sharpen him in the Lord. Someone with a passion in his heart and fire in his mouth. Someone willing to risk it all for Jesus. Someone whom I could study the Word with, pray with, and worship with. I've always had a huge heart for worship and have such joy expressing my love for the Lord through worship, and as a musician, it would be icing on the cake if he were also musical.

But William wasn't any of those things, yet I rationalized someday he could be. But how long would that take? In other situations in life, having faith for miracles is good, but when it comes to missionary dating, it's not a good idea. Because when you play with fire, chances are, you'll get burned.

No matter how many assumptions and rationalizations I made, I couldn't deny the Holy Spirit's whispers. But I still ignored them. And I ignored all my friends. And all my family. You'd think having the advice of those I loved, trusted, and respected most would have motivated me to break up with William again. But I delayed. Every day was an internal struggle because I just couldn't let go of him.

How could something so seemingly obvious and simple be so difficult? Because my heart and emotions were involved, tangled up in a romance with a non-Christian at the same time my Lover and Lord was trying to woo me with His love.

I had a few friends tell me they felt the Lord was jealous of this relationship and even told me that if I didn't end it, He would. That the Lord was so in love with me and missed those intimate times together, but I was using up that time with this boy instead. I thought I could have both God and him, but I couldn't.

Not only was I spending less time with the Lord, but my moral lines were being challenged. Bad company *corrupts* good character. God said it, so it's true. But I had thought that good company could *change* bad character.

As someone who didn't drink, I understood that finding someone with my views was unlikely, so it didn't surprise me that William drank or that he drunk-texted me during the first week of our communication. Or the times when I didn't hear from him (since we talked quite often), that he was drunk. Those should have been not only red flags, but they should have been stop signs. But I was smitten and infatuated, so I turned a blind eye and even laughed it off.

But after I met William, the chemistry I felt was like nothing I'd ever experienced before. And it made me very curious if I would like kissing him. So after only a week, and on our first date no less, when he slowly started to come in for a kiss, I let him and discovered there was nothing wrong with me. I was definitely human. Too human. Since he wasn't a Christian, he tried pushing the boundaries. He saw my hesitancy because I moved away when his hands started to wander. He apologized. And then I rationalized— he wasn't saved, so he just didn't know better. But I knew better. When he apologized, he seemed genuinely sorry that he had gotten caught up in the moment. I apologized that I hadn't been clearer where my boundaries were.

*A most powerful message.*

The most imperative, important time I broke up with him was because I couldn't ignore the Lord anymore. After breaking up the first time, I'd received a prophetic word that I had stepped out of the covering of the Lord (as seen in a vision of something that looked like a glass house surrounding me). That vision rang true because I knew I had indeed stepped out of God's will.

And also because seven years prior, I'd seen that glass covering of protection in a vision, written it down, but not told anyone. Rereading it, the Lord had said it was specifically protection against men who might try to pursue me but who weren't for me. He told me that no one could get inside of that shield, but I could step out. Gulp. I had.

Even though I'd stepped back in after breaking up with William, we started talking again. And I knew I'd stepped out again. This protection was also favor of the Lord. And walking out of that made me susceptible to not only confusion and deception, but physical illness. I was on a trip for work when I got sick.

On top of that, I got extremely painful hemorrhoids that made it difficult to even walk. And I remember late at night hobbling around in my hotel room while not being able to sleep because of the pain, compounded by the sickness.

And even in excruciating pain, I saw my situation so clearly. I knew what I had to do. The Lord was speaking so clearly through the pain I was experiencing. So I left William a text (since I'd already broken up with him conventionally, I assumed a text was acceptable). I knew he would be in a cabin in Alaska without cell service for days. And since he wouldn't get it until later, I hoped he might not respond. And he didn't . . . for six days.

When he did respond, he said he didn't understand. He thought things were going well again. So of course, I tried my best to explain, but by the end of the evening, he still didn't understand and I had to say the breakup goodbye again. We continued the conversation of his not understanding what I was talking about until I had hemorrhoid surgery and was recovering.

During this period, I used the time to spend with the Lord. And it was so refreshing. I felt closer to Him than I had in a long time. His presence was so strong that I wanted nothing else than to be with Him. And through those intimate times with my Forever Love, I knew what I had to do (again).

This time, I recorded a video, since that was as close as I could get to face to face. And in it, I shared with William my heart for the Lord, my love for Him, and my passion for Him. And why I couldn't have both God and him.

But William's response surprised me. He said he felt vilified from my having to choose between him and the Holy Spirit. I assured him that my intention was not to make him feel that way but to only explain more.

His response was "I don't get it."

And I realized something: that was exactly why I had to end things again. If he truly "got it," we wouldn't be having this conversation because we would have been on the same page spiritually. And then, after all my explaining, he finally said, "No need to explain more—I concede."

After I finally had ripped that figurative bandage off as the Lord instructed, I was about a week into my recovery from the surgery. The doctor had said that I would always have loose, flabby skin where the hemorrhoid had been. And also that the long incision mark would become a scar. I didn't care because obviously no one would be seeing it.

Miraculously, after I had ended things with William, the recovery pain I had been experiencing immediately subsided. In my curiosity, I checked the incision mark. It was gone, completely gone. And the flabby skin was now taut. The loose skin and incision mark had been there the day before. But it was as if my obedience to the

Lord prompted His instant healing of the external wound. I was then able to go right back to work.

*Curveball.*

I was finally doing well. I had even dated a little. It had been nine months since our final breakup. I saw William from time to time at the Boise airport, and our relationship had been congenial. I didn't let myself text him because I knew the pain that would ensue if I let myself go there.

Then, out of the blue, William texted me. My heart rate quickened, not from excitement but from nervous concern at what his message said. He asked how I liked living in southern Oregon because he was thinking about applying for a position at the airport I was based out of.

He was born and raised in Boise, attended college there, and owned a home about five minutes from his parents. The thought of him picking up and moving to Oregon seemed preposterous. But it was also unexpectedly endearing. I couldn't help but wonder if a part of him wanted to move to my town for me. He didn't know anyone else there. So I was completely flattered.

After I put aside the warm feelings, I quickly came to my senses. I couldn't have him living in my town. I couldn't see him at the airport every time I went to work. And I most certainly couldn't have the temptation of his attractive self in such close proximity. I trusted my decision and my resolve when he was far away in Boise but immediately questioned my ability to resist him if he was living close.

So I put my walls of defenses up and texted him back, trying to convince him that moving would be a bad idea, and I wouldn't be able to be his friend or even have any communication with him whatsoever (outside of what our jobs required).

He seemed a little offended at that and told me that his moving was just something he had to do for himself. So I backed off and stopped texting him.

When he texted me saying he got the job, I congratulated him on the outside, but on the inside, I was trembling over what it would be like to see him again. I was so torn up by emotion. So I told him we could try being friends. Nothing more, nothing less. I thought perhaps that might be possible. But then just a couple weeks after his arrival, he kissed me. . . Before, his kiss had been enrapturing; now, confusion filled my senses.

All I felt was guilt. I realized that my emotions refused to surrender to him because I knew better now. I knew we had no future, so I stopped underestimating my ability to say no to the lie that I would never feel for anyone else what I'd felt for him. I knew he didn't have a superpower that sucked me under his spell. I was fully capable of saying no to his charms.

After that revelation, I made certain he knew we couldn't cross that line again. And we could not physically "hang out" after work. I would love to tell you that this was the end of the saga. But it did become more complicated.

Months later, William texted me that he had received word his grandfather had passed away in Boise. He was devastated and obviously missing having family near. So he asked if he might accompany me to church, because he wanted to find closure with his grandfather's death.

Internally, I tried to calm the hope that rose in my throat as I saw him walk in the doors of my church. It was like a dream coming true.

After the service, my pastor walked over and introduced himself to William.

I was conversing with a sweet lady but kept stealing glances at what was happening several feet away. I couldn't believe my eyes. William's head was bowed. And my pastor had his arm around his shoulder as he led William in the prayer of salvation.

My heart was so happy. It had been a year and a half since I first met William, and in that time, I never dreamt I would see this happen right in front of me.

There was just one problem. William was now dating a girl from Boise. As you can imagine, I was so torn inside. Did William know that what happened at church that day made a way for us to date again? Yet I couldn't say anything with him dating another girl.

## My Waiting Takeaway

As I sought the Lord through this new development and worshipped, prayed, and wrote in my journal a lot, I realized some earth-shattering revelations.

*Lesson 1: I was not actually in love with William.*

And I never was. You may be just as shocked as I was to discover that. I had romanticized the notion of love because I craved his attention. My desire grew exponentially because he was forbidden. Why do we always want what we cannot have? It's part of our sin-nature.

Once I recognized that it wasn't love but lust that drew me to him, I started analyzing my relationship with him and what drove me. I had believed the lie that he was the only one for me. And I believed the lie that I would never feel that way about anyone ever again.

I can now say without a doubt that those were absolute lies, because the intensity and depth of the sacrificial love I feel for my husband doesn't even come close to the selfish lust I had felt for William.

I believe that the enemy put William in my path to get me off track and to get me to stop believing in the promises of God over my life. There were times it almost worked. But God always prevailed.

*Lesson 2: God is my strength.*

After going through those trials, I came out stronger than I have ever been. I was so weak and human during those times, but God showed Himself as strong. And now I know that all my strength comes from Him. He is the reason I can overcome. He is the reason I come home to an amazing, God-fearing, God-loving, selfless, kindhearted, wonderful man every night. I can't take any credit for that!

*Lesson 3: What surrender truly means.*

The other consequence the enemy hadn't counted on me learning was what true surrender is. It isn't something I can conjure up of my own accord. It is relinquishing my will to the Father (with His help) and exchanging it for His perfect will. In the moment, God's perfect will can feel like sacrifice of something I desperately want; but in the end, I was sacrificing something not good for me. If I hadn't sacrificed my desire for William, I would have never married my amazing husband.

*Lesson 4: Christ will help me overcome.*

So whatever happened to William? Well, after I came to those life-changing conclusions, the enemy had one last-ditch effort up his sleeve to see if he could throw me off. Some months after accepting Christ, William, who was dating the gal from Boise, sent me a text that essentially asked for an inappropriate photo. I was dismayed. Did he honestly think I was that type of girl?

I typed back a frustrated message relaying my disappointment that he would even ask, and instantly lost all respect for this man I had unrightfully idolized. And in that moment, I realized the Lord was showing me why He gave me an escape from this relationship.

I asked him if he meant it when he had accepted Christ into his life. His response was that he had felt cornered and didn't want to let anyone down. So there it was. The truth. Had I known that at the time, it would have saved me from a lot of unnecessary heartache and frustration. William seemed to recognize that he had lost all hope of any sort of future with me and completely stopped any sort of pursuit after that.

*Lesson 5: Dating an unbeliever will cause your relationship with God to slip.*

I didn't see it then, but my relationship with the Lord was slipping away as my relationship with him grew. And that is the normal progression of entertaining a relationship with someone who isn't a believer. I slowly, almost unknowingly, began to lose my closeness with the Lord.

*Lesson 6: I want to save the physical aspects of a relationship for my future husband.*

I shouldn't have been kissing William at all. I'm the girl who saved her first kiss until twenty-five years of age. And then, I let a non-Christian kiss me after knowing him for just one week. I remember feeling so disappointed in myself. But I learned from this that the more physical a relationship is, the harder it is to pull free from the emotional soul ties it creates. Because of that, my heart bore the brunt of it. Each sweet, affectionate, endearing word he wrote would eventually become knives in my heart.

*Lesson 7: I want to learn from my past, but not change it.*

In retrospect, I am glad I went through every emotion that I did because every victory made me a little stronger in my faith, and every trial and temptation showed me that even when my selfish, stubborn will is screaming loudest, Christ will still help me overcome in the end.

I knew this meant waiting longer for marriage. But I decided I wanted to keep waiting with patient expectation. I wouldn't settle. I would wait until I felt the Lord was giving the green light and His blessing before entering into marriage.

I started to pray diligently that the Lord would bless the man I was to marry, that He would keep him from harm and keep him surrounded by His awesome, unfathomable love. And when the day arrived, I found that my future husband had prayed the same prayer for me.

### Your Waiting Step

Here are some words of caution and encouragement for your next steps.

*Caution*

**Don't make excuses for inappropriate behavior.**

When William groped me, I mentally made the excuse that he didn't know any better. But the bottom line is, as Christians, we know better. So date men who know better and will respect you as an unmarried woman.

**Ask questions instead of making assumptions.**

Had I asked William about his apparent conversion to Christianity right after it had happened, I would have known that he was only doing what he thought was expected. Knowing the answers to deal-breaker questions can be hard, but it's very necessary.

*Encouragement*

**God will always help you overcome.**

But He also wants you to seek Him out. Surrender selfishness and remind yourself who you are in Him, and humbly lift your heart to the one who already holds it in His hands.

**Ask the Lord to show you what surrender should look like in your life.**

Is there a relationship that needs to be surrendered? What desires do you want to set down and ask God to replace with His desires?

**Remember that He is worth every sacrifice.**

Sacrifices seem so hard in the moment of decision, but when put in perspective, any sacrifice you and I can make is nothing compared to the sacrifice He made. His love is worth more than anything you may have to surrender.

**Remember that God will often use your greatest struggle and turn it into your greatest victory and testimony.**

If you take anything away from my stories, it's this: Put God first, very first, and then you'll know what your other priorities should be. Then trust Him. And don't settle.

And it's unbelievably amazing to think that His sacrifice was for you and me.

## Your Waiting Journal Tips

Brainstorm some areas where you are not putting God first. Can you write about the areas of your life where you are tightly holding onto the reins? Now, think about surrendering those over to the Lord. And as you do, let His sweet love pour over you. Ask Him to exchange your plans for His divine plan to unfold in your life.

## Verse and Prayer

"Do not be yoked together with unbelievers. For what do righteousness and wickedness have in common? Or what fellowship can light have with darkness? What harmony is there between Christ and Belial? Or what does a believer have in common with an unbeliever? What agreement is there between the temple of God and idols? For we are the temple of the living God." (2 Cor. 6:14–16 NIV)

*Father God, I pray* that I will not ever choose to be yoked to an unbeliever. If I am ever tempted in this, please show me right away. And if I am currently in an unequally yoked relationship, please provide a way out. And heal my heart. Help me to keep my head on straight in relationships. I want a clear head. I pray that I won't get tangled in emotions and lust with a man who is not for me. Please keep the hands of ungodly men far from me. And help me have the patience to wait for my future husband, physically and emotionally. In Your name. Amen.

# I WAS NEVER A
# MORNING PERSON

I'd become accustomed to singleness . . .
Not to say I didn't want to experience
the oneness of having a husband.
But I didn't let my heart stray to wistfulness . . . often.
On occasion, I'd wonder what wedded bliss consisted
of—
Did it liken to a love song, story, or script?
Or was it a disappointing, disillusioned detachment
from the romanticized versions displayed in film and
literature?
And then one day, I tied the knot—
with a three-cord strand that bound me unwaveringly
to him.
Beforehand, I was never a morning person.
Before coffee meant before coherence,
where grunts took the place of words and sentences.
But now, mornings are my favorite.
That moment my cognizance awakens

and my eyelids begin to open,
I see his perfect sleeping form curled up next to me.
I slowly reach to touch his face
with the nimbleness you'd use
to brush a petal with your fingertips.
When he doesn't wake, I curl up closer
until I feel his skin against my skin.
And I smile in wonderment at this heaven that I'm in.
I close my eyes in a prayer of thanks.
Then I doze a little longer.
Until excitement fills my being
when I feel his breathing soften
and his arms tighten in embrace.
He's awake!
This man I've pledged my life to
looks adoringly at me
with intense green eyes
that smile straight into my soul.
And every morning I have this thought—
how can he look so dashingly handsome
first thing in the morning?!
You'd think it'd make me insecure
of the tangled mess splayed across my face.
But by the look in his eyes,
you'd think it was his first time
looking at his bride.
I used to dread mornings—
the monotony, the messy hair in the mirror,
the groggy grumpiness,
and the apparent singleness.
But now, tasting this bliss
and seeing his unshakable, unbreakable love
makes me marvel as I revel in the parallel:
This must be the earthly representation of Christ's love
for me.

## — I Was Never a Morning Person —

And I realize how my husband rises to the challenge—
to love me as Christ loves the church
from the second he awakes—
which is why mornings
are now my favorite time of day.

# Chapter 12

## MY LOVE STORY

Jesus is the most patient individual in history . . . *ever*. When He created the world, He knew that thousands of years later He would have to die a horrific death. And yet He waited. When He was born, He knew He had thirty-three years to walk the earth before He died. But He did it. And after He rose from the grave, He knew He would be waiting thousands of years more before He would be reunited with His bride. The foretold wedding feast of the Lamb has yet to happen, and still, He waits patiently.

Our brief lives are a vapor compared to the lengths He's waited. If we can just be reminded of this eternal perspective, maybe then we can try to be more like Jesus, patiently waiting for our wedding: whether it happens here on earth or once we're swept up with our Bridegroom who awaits our arrival in heaven.

### My Waiting Story

During my time of singleness, I felt like I'd heard a lifetime of people's unsolicited thoughts about my dating life. For every piece of good advice, there was a contradictory one. My initial response was always to grin and bear it. So ultimately, I had to take those questions to the Lord to see what His advice for me was.

But the advice went deeper than the comments. It was their underlying supposition that I would not be happy, fulfilled, or completed until I found a mate. And this even came from those in turbulent relationships, which made even less sense to me since I was considerably more "happy" in my singleness then they were in a relationship. Why? I came to the realization that waiting didn't have to equate pining. Pining is the consequence of unbelief in God's promises. Instead, we should wait in the way God intended us to wait—patiently.

I like the Greek definition of waiting, which is to welcome from the heart a future outcome, to expect, to look for, to await. I call that waiting with patient expectation.

What does that look like? Paul describes it beautifully, calling us to be "joyful in hope, patient in affliction, and faithful in prayer" (Rom. 12:12 NIV).

*Where it started.*

As I hinted at earlier, my husband was friends with my brother first. I met Kevin after he and my brother became friends during their freshman year of high school. I was a few years older than them. So Kevin was just my little brother's outgoing friend. As you are probably assuming, there was nothing romantic between the two of us for many years!

During high school, I knew Kevin's sister, Kaitlin. In their family, they were more than siblings, but friends—just as I was with my siblings. That being the case, there were times over the years after high school when we'd all get together with a group of friends and siblings to have movie or game nights and even tailgate to drive-ins.

But then I became a flight attendant and moved away for a few years. I didn't go to any more of their fun events, but eventually, I transferred up to the flight attendant base in Portland, Oregon, just an hour from where I grew up.

One week later, after writing a blog post about being content in singleness, I received this Facebook message from Kaitlin: "I recently had the thought—why hadn't I tried setting you up with a certain someone? I even talked to my mom about it today, and she said you had recently come to mind too. I haven't talked to this certain somebody about you yet, but are you opposed to being set up?"

I responded promptly: "Hey Kaitlin! I'm not opposed to being set up at all. Though I should mention that the last time I was set up a couple years ago, the guy turned out to be struggling with being gay. And even though we gave it a shot, his preference for males ended up being a big reason we ended it. Hope you and your family are well!"

She responded just as quickly: "Ok, thank you for sharing that! Man, what an experience! Sounds like an episode of a TV show! Ok, so the guy I have in mind is actually my brother! He's in management at a grocery store now and graduated college debt free, moving out into his own place, and I think he's quite the catch. And well, of course, if things went well, I'd love you as a sister-in-law! Still interested in having me try to set something up?"

After the initial shock subsided, I thought about it. I would have never considered Kevin. He was my little brother's best friend. Wasn't he still pretty much a boy? I had to remind myself that he was then a twenty-six-year-old man.

I responded: "Your brother does seem like a great guy! Though I don't think he'd be interested, since I am older. It's been my observation that age tends to be a bigger deal for guys when the girl is older."

She answered: "Well, I'll discreetly put some feelers out. I do know age wouldn't matter to him since he had a crush on an older girl a few years back, but the age difference was an issue for her! Haha. But yes, generally that does bother guys!"

I said: "Haha, ok, you can feel free to put your feelers out!"

Literally the very next day, I had another message from Kaitlin. "He would love to get together and see if you and he might like to explore dating together. I'd love to have you and Kevin over for dinner to take some of the pressure off, and you guys can just kinda see if you have enough in common to say, 'Let's meet again!' When will you be in Salem next?"

We continued to communicate over the phone and set up the double date for that week.

Before I knew it, I was standing in Kaitlin's living room, wearing jeans, cowboy boots, and one of my favorite blue shirts. I doubt Kevin remembers what I was wearing. But when he recounts the story, he says that as soon as he came in, he saw me in a new light. And as I turned around when he walked in the door, my hair flounced to the side, and he was in awe. (His words, of course.)

And when he walked in, the first thing I noticed was his work uniform, which looked particularly dashing on him. I realized that seeing him in uniform was good—for me to actually see him as a working adult rather than a little high schooler. Even though he'd been employed throughout the previous ten years, seeing him in uniform assured me he had indeed grown up. And he immediately looked like a handsome man rather than the scrawny boy I remembered.

As soon as we started to reconnect, it became apparent to Kaitlin and her husband that they were no longer needed. So they excused themselves to put the kids to bed. I wondered why it took them so long to put their kids down. But of course, we found out later, they were just giving us time to chat since they couldn't get a word in edgewise.

As we were chatting, Kevin mentioned that something was located in a different "quadrant" from his neighborhood.

I raised my eyebrows and asked, "Quadrant? Like from *Star Trek*?"

His eyes lit up. "Yes! Do you like *Star Trek*?"

"Yes! I grew up watching it. I'm currently rewatching the *Next Generation*."

Kevin's jaw dropped. "You're kidding! I own every *Next Generation* episode. I'm currently rewatching *Voyager*."

"No way! I love *Voyager* too!" How did I not know he was a "trekkie" like my brother and me?

Kevin and I continued chatting about other things and quickly realized that we had much, much more in common than we had thought. We were completely taken by surprise by all of our similarities.

As he walked me to my car that night, he fumbled with his phone, explaining that he had to get a new one and had lost all his contacts. After a little more nervous explaining, I soon realized he was asking for my number since it was no longer in his phone.

He clarified further: "Because I'd like to take you to dinner and a movie if you would be up for it?"

I was so thankful that he made his intentions perfectly apparent. There was no guessing that he wanted to go on another date. I would have said yes even if I didn't want to, because men don't do that anymore! Hanging out isn't a date. Going to coffee isn't a date—unless they clarify that it is. Even inviting someone to lunch isn't an obvious date. But dinner and a movie—now that's a good, old-fashioned date! I was thrilled. With all the dating I had done, I'd never been asked out like that.

My next step was a little nerve-wracking because I had to go to my brother and ask what he thought. My brother was a little surprised that Kevin hadn't talked to him about it first. So I told him that if he wasn't in favor of it or if it would be awkward, I would not go on that next date. I would rather snip it early before our feelings became too involved.

But my brother shook his head. He said that it might be a little weird at first. Then he said, "You guys are perfect for each other. You're like the same person, just a different gender."

After our first dinner date (which was with his parents), the movie, and then another group date with a bunch of his friends (who all approved, by the way), he took me out to restaurants, and then hiking, to the coast, more hiking, more dinners and movies, and pretty soon, I fell in love.

I didn't allow myself to fall for him right away because I had experienced so many failed relationships. And I had my list. So I would email him a set of questions. And each dinner date, he would bring them, printed off with his answers. I was shocked because his answers were exactly what I was looking for.

I remember going back to my apartment and typing on my computer, trying to come up with more and more questions. After I had already sent all my normal questions, I was wracking my brain for more to ask. My confidant roommate, Katie, saw my frustration. She said, "Jolene, you have asked that poor boy so many personal questions. Have you considered that you might not actually have any more questions to ask?"

I pondered her question. She was right. I had asked everything I had to ask. And he had answered my deal-breaker questions beautifully. At that point, I prayed and told the Lord that I'd see where He led this relationship and would now sit back and just enjoy the ride.

It became difficult not to tell him that I loved him. On one particular drive to the beach in Astoria, Oregon, to see Fort Stevens, I told the Lord silently, *If he doesn't tell me he loves me TODAY, I am going to tell him. Okay? But please, just let him say it first.*

Even though it was purely my own impatience, the Lord honored my request. That day, Kevin wrote his name in the sand and then mine with a heart between us. I didn't let him off the hook that easily. "What does that mean?"

His sweet, simple answer was, "It means I love you, Jolene."

I thanked the Lord in my heart as I told Kevin I loved him too.

## My Waiting Takeaway

Throughout the time Kevin and I dated, the Lord showed me in several ways that we were meant for each other. I started keeping track of the confirmations.

*First confirmation: the unexpected book.*

After we had both shared that we were in love with each other, I soon realized that I not only loved him, but that I wanted to marry him. The realization prompted me to look into something. My mom had given me a book, *Praying for Your Husband from Head to Toe*, several months prior. I found it again and noticed she had written a note on the inside cover: *I know this seems a little odd. But I felt like I was supposed to give this to you because whether you find your husband in a week or a year from now, the greatest gift you can give to him is to pray for him.*

She had dated her note May 25—the day after Kevin and I had gone on our first double date. Some may call it coincidence, but I like to call coincidences "God winks" (coined by Squire Rushnell). When you have asked the Lord for a confirmation, there is no such thing as a simple coincidence.

As the months passed by, we began discussing marriage. Kevin made certain I knew that he was serious about marrying me. After about a week of the subject coming up here and there, I began to wonder when he would kiss me (since I'd also told him that I didn't want him to kiss me until he knew he wanted to marry me).

And now that it was apparent he was planning to, I started getting a bit anxious, wanting to finally kiss my love. We had been giving each other pecks on the cheek of late, and he was getting dangerously close to my lips, which only intensified my desire.

One day as we were watching a movie, he leaned over and planted a couple soft kisses against my cheek. I didn't know if he realized it or not, but one of his kisses strayed to the corner of my mouth. At that point, I could hardly handle the suspense and blurted, "You know my stipulation for kissing me is you have to plan to marry me, and we have been discussing marriage lately. So you could—"

Before I even finished my sentence, Kevin's lips covered mine. I closed my eyes, reveling in the beauty and newness of our first kiss. And yes, I was relieved to find I thoroughly enjoyed kissing him.

*Second confirmation: from argument to prophetic confirmation.*

As our discussions about marriage continued, Kevin took me ring shopping to see what styles I liked. I had even started planning—looking at flowers and bridesmaid dresses.

Things were progressing nicely until one day we had our first dating disagreement. It was about video games. I had told him that I didn't have positive feelings toward the topic because of stories I'd heard from friends over the years whose husbands were so addicted the women felt like their husband's second wife.

Kevin assured me that he didn't have an addiction, although at one point during high school, he did. That fact made me worry that even if it wasn't currently, it could become a problem again. And I shared that concern with him.

It was hard for me to accept that someone could have a healthy relationship with video games. And since Kevin had his weekly Wednesday video gaming night with the guys, it made me question if that was a nonnegotiable commitment or if he would ever take a week off for a vacation or date night. And I suddenly wondered how often during the week he played.

Since I'd never dated someone who played video games, it hadn't been on my list of questions, so I broached the subject.

Emotions were high for both of us because we knew we wanted to get married, and we'd never faced anything we disagreed on. He insisted again that he didn't have a problem with them. I had to accept that even though it was difficult.

Feeling the weight of having our first disagreement, I started to question what I already knew—that I was supposed to marry him. It may seem like a silly thing to consider cause for alarm. But up to that point, if I'd come across what I deemed a major disagreement with a date, I would break up with the guy.

But I knew in my heart, this relationship was different, and this man was different from any I had dated before. So I reached out to a family friend for prayer. She didn't know Kevin and I were discussing marriage or that we just had a disagreement, and I didn't tell her. She was a very prophetic woman of God, so I wanted to let God speak through her about the issue.

And speak He did. The first thing she told me when she started praying was "Don't worry; the plans you are making are good." As I thought about the wedding plans I had just been brainstorming, she said that she saw me in a white dress and that it was about to be the most exciting time I've had in my life.

It was just the confirmation I was looking for. Hearing those words calmed my anxious heart and filled it with peace once again.

After our initial disagreement, Kevin and I had sort of agreed to disagree on the subject of video games, particularly violent video games. But soon, I started noticing that Kevin would not go to the guys' video game night in favor of taking me out on a date. I wondered if the trend would continue once in a while.

Soon he told me that if we both weren't working on a Wednesday night, then the night belonged to us. I felt so loved and cherished that he would do that for me. And eventually, Kevin casually told me he was selling one of his gaming systems and the games that went along with it. When I asked him why, he responded that he'd been thinking about raising children and that he didn't want to have any violent video games in the house. Internally, I was ecstatic. But then, collecting myself, I assured him I was completely in favor of his decision.

This situation made me realize that even though we can have disagreements, respecting each other's point of view is necessary and vital in a relationship. If I hadn't expressed myself in a respectful way, I doubt Kevin would have listened to my point of view. When someone is defensive with us, our gut instinct is to be defensive back, but Proverbs 15:1 says, "A gentle answer turns away wrath."

I can't stress enough how important this verse is in relationships because I think that reacting harshly is never warranted. There have been times when my knee-jerk reaction would be to react defensively with Kevin, but after I take a moment to think about how to word what I'm feeling in a respectful way, his response is never harsh. And I often find that the reason I thought I had for wanting to be defensive in the first place was based on a misunderstanding. How embarrassing it would have been to react harshly only to find out that it was completely unwarranted.

*Third confirmation: an offer of free music.*

After we became engaged, Kevin and I started discussing when to have the wedding. It was an easy decision. I had vacation time off in May (over five months away), which would be the only way I could guarantee being off work for our honeymoon. Otherwise, we would have to wait about a year and a half. That was just too long.

We quickly decided, and plans were underway. We had already secured a florist and cake decorator without even having to look around. As a manager of a grocery store, Kevin was friends with employees from all the departments. And both the florist and cake decorator offered their services at cost! We were pleasantly surprised and thankful.

I tried not to think much about the music, but I knew I wouldn't be able to avoid it forever. My dad brought it up one day. He suggested the famous Pachelbel's Canon for the processional.

I shook my head without even considering the possibility. "No, I've played that on my violin for so many weddings over the years. I'd probably be critiquing whoever plays it."

"There isn't anyone?" my dad asked.

"The only one I would trust to play it would be Valerie!" I hadn't meant to suggest my old high school friend and orchestra comrade as an option, but I just blurted it out.

"Why don't you ask her?"

"I haven't seen her in eleven years! There's no way I could just call her out of nowhere and ask her to play at my wedding."

Yes, she was an amazing violinist even back in high school. And she was our director's daughter. Thinking more about it, I remembered that she was going to major in music, which made me wonder how amazing she was after all those years.

Later that evening while out to dinner with my fiancé, I told Kevin about my dad's suggestion. He thought it was a great idea. I, on the other hand, still did not. "It would be embarrassing after all these years . . ."

Before I went to bed that night, I prayed a quick prayer that God's will would be done regarding the music.

The very next morning, I got a Facebook message. My heart nearly froze when I saw it was from Valerie. There's no way my dad or Kevin would have known how to contact her—plus, neither of them even had a Facebook account!

I immediately opened the message. Instantly, I saw a photo of the two of us from after we graduated. It was from Vienna, Austria, where our orchestra took part in an international competition. She wrote: "Hi, Jolene! This popped up on my news feed this morning as having been posted eleven years ago today. Time flies! I hope you are doing well. That was such a fun trip!"

I was dumbfounded. Squealing in delight, I wrote get back as quickly as my fingers could type. I asked how she was as well. And then I told her I was getting married in May and wondered if she would be willing to play for the wedding, specifically Pachelbel's Canon.

Her response was: "Oh my! Congratulations, Jolene! That is so exciting to be planning a wedding. I would absolutely *love* to play in your wedding. Let me know if you have any more special requests! And since you are a friend, it won't cost a thing! Life is good right now. I am halfway through my doctorate in performance. Your fiancé is a very lucky man!"

A doctorate in music performance? I was truly thrilled. I'd be having a professional violinist willing to play at my wedding for free, and she was an old friend!

If that had been the end of it, I still would have been ecstatic. But a couple weeks later, Kevin was working at the grocery store when he ran into Mr. Nelson, my old music instructor. Kevin was excited to see him since he'd known him from high school symphony too. He said, "Mr. Nelson! I hear your daughter is playing at my wedding!"

Mr. Nelson responded, "She is? Who are you marrying?"

"Jolene!"

"Oh, that's wonderful, Kevin! You know, if you would like, I'd be honored to play with her at your wedding too."

So we had two amazing violinists: a father-daughter duo playing at our wedding! It was such a God-wink, further confirming that He was blessing our coming union.

*A promise of forever.*

Wedding planning went so smoothly. I was amazed because I had been warned by numerous people to be prepared for hiccups and issues. But I was thankful to bypass those.

Our wedding day was perfect in my eyes. It was supposed to be a rainy day in May. But the sun peeked through the morning clouds as we had our photos taken outside. We weren't hit by a drop of rain all morning.

The ceremony and reception were inside the church we now attend. My grandfather and our pastor both took part in our ceremony.

Kevin and I wrote our own vows and somehow managed to not share them with each other beforehand. I say "somehow" because we have the hardest time keeping surprises a secret.

My eyes watered when Kevin read his vows to me. Here's a meaningful snippet from his vows to me:

> "When I close my eyes, all I can think about is how perfect you are: your eyes, your smile, your heart . . . everything about you is amazing and I count myself extremely blessed to be marrying you today. With great anticipation, I look forward to spending the rest of my life with you and I want you to know that I will always be there for you, both in times of happiness and laughter and times of sadness . . . It'll be my greatest joy to be by your side for the rest of my life!"

And then my eyes watered again as I attempted to read my vows to him—this amazing man whom I had waited thirty years for. I was so excited to spend the rest of my life with him. Here's the last part of my vows to him:

"I will pray that my love for you will be ever growing and ever-maturing. And I'll pray that I will love you with the love that Christ loves you with—that sacrificial, pure, unselfish, devoted, radical, and fierce love of God. If I could but see a glimpse of His love for you, how could I not treat you as the son of the Most High King?! Kevin, you are the most treasured gift God has ever bestowed upon me. And today, I promise you the rest of my life!"

After the reception, as we ran out to his car with birdseed flying at us in farewell, the rain still didn't come. But almost immediately, as we started driving away, the Lord let the rains come for the rest of the day. I was so thankful. We were able to have the outdoor photos we wanted. Then, to have the rain begin as soon as we left the reception just felt like God was smiling down on our new marriage.

**Your Waiting Step**

There are things you can do while waiting for God to bring the right man your way.

*Pray for absolute clarity regarding God's will for your life.*

The act of prayer is important because God loves it when you bring your heart before Him. It also is important because prayer brings peace. The more you pray about stressful situations or concerns, the more peace and contentment you will feel in the midst of the current storms. That's because it's an exchange of giving your worries to the Lord and Him replacing them with His love and direction.

*Keep your heart and mind pure as you wait.*

Purity, either physical or emotional, can be a gift you give to your husband. Impurity creates baggage that can cause difficulties in marriage. Instead, be intentional about the way you live your physical life and thought life to keep an action and attitude of purity.

*Again, guard your heart in the waiting.*

A part of that is guarding your emotions so you don't get swept away by infatuation. If you protect your heart, you will be able to better discern what you want and don't want in a spouse because you won't stay long in a dead-end relationship.

Ask the Lord if His clarity in this equates to marrying a godly man or living a single life devoted to the Lord. And remember, He can give you peace in whatever stage of life He has you in.

**Your Waiting Journal Tips**

Write a poem or letter for your future husband that you can one day give to him. Also write a poem to your first love, Jesus Christ. You can touch on how you are being patient in waiting, how you will always put Christ first, and that you are confident in God's perfect plan for your life.

**Verse and Prayer**

"Take delight in the Lord, and He will give you the desires of your heart." (Ps. 37:4 NIV)

*Dear Lord, thank You* so very much that You have my best interests at heart. I praise You for Your goodness in my life. And I thank You that no matter what Your plan is for my life, it will be good. I will choose to have peace over anxiety. And I will choose to delight in You every day of my life.

# ONE DAY

One day I'll see your face
and know there'll be no other.
One day I'll turn away
from every other lover.
But for now your aura's a blank canvas,
your face an empty mass,
while your stature, I can only envision
through my endless imagination.
I don't know if you'll be handsome
by the standards of the world,
but I know you'll be
inevitably
attractive to me.
I know you won't be perfect;
you'll falter, fail, and fall,
but I'll love you even still . . .
Because I'm just as foolishly flawed
and inevitably human
as the man I'll one day wed.

# Chapter 13

## BANISH EXPECTATIONS
## OF PERFECTION

When Kevin started college, he began studying meteorology, but after several advanced calculus courses, he lost interest. After brainstorming, he decided to change his major to education and focus on becoming a high school history teacher. Yet after two terms of student teaching, he determined that teaching was not for him.

He decided to major in history and began taking business classes for his minor. He quickly discovered he devoured the content and had a natural business mindset. So after graduating, he decided to continue working his way up in management in grocery, using the business aspect of his degree. Because of the detours, it took him longer to complete college. Yet even though life took unexpected turns, he grew through learning various studies and gained insight into where he excelled.

Life won't ever be perfect. Our expectations of a perfect relationship or marriage are unrealistic, similar to expecting life to unfold in a certain way. And when something doesn't go in a way we consider "perfect," it just shows the adventure of life. The unexpected nature of life makes it interesting and exciting.

## My Waiting Story

Even though I had a plethora of confirmations that I was supposed to marry Kevin, and even though I know we are a perfect match for each other, that doesn't mean either of us is perfect.

We don't always communicate perfectly. We sometimes inadvertently hurt each other. We sometimes have miscommunications. We are sometimes tired, hungry, or grumpy. But when those times happen and one of us apologizes to the other for our un-Christlike behavior, the other will accept that apology with the reminder that we're only human. We know that we aren't perfect. We sometimes forget events or groceries. As humans, we are prone to make mistakes.

As such, we have to remember to be forgiving when one of us acts like a human. Because when it's Kevin, I have to remember, it could just as easily have been me. We have to remind ourselves to be soft, gentle, and always forgiving. And when we treat one another with that kind of respect, we find that the frequency of our miscommunications and hurts becomes less and less. Now, similar to going into marriage without expectations that life will be perfect, it's prudent to have that outlook for your wedding and honeymoon as well.

I went into my wedding day expecting rain and expecting any number of things to go awry, which could have easily happened. I praise God that they didn't.

But our honeymoon, on the other hand, was nothing like I expected it to be. When you've waited thirty years to have sexual intimacy with the love of God's choice for your life, you go into your honeymoon expecting some surreal, earth-shaking experience. Thankfully, I was able to easily let go of all unrealistic expectations of our honeymoon and was able to enjoy every exciting new adventure with my husband.

I remember when we had landed in Hawaii and Kevin called the hotel asking about a shuttle. He started to explain, "My fianc—I mean, my *wife* and I just arrived . . ." The fact that we could now call each other husband and wife surprised and delighted us both. I recall standing there, smiling in pride as he called me his wife for the very first time. We were staring at each other with goofy grins, ogling into each other's eyes.

Little did we know what an adventure our honeymoon would be. I have heard so many crazy honeymoon stories that I am convinced God has a sense of humor.

On our second night in our Honolulu hotel room, we were getting ready for bed after a fun, exhausting day at Pearl Harbor. Kevin came out of the bathroom and quickly shut the door. "Maybe they'll just stay in there."

"*They* who?" I asked, instantly more awake.

Kevin sighed. "There are some cockroaches that scattered when I turned the light on."

"Oh no. Can we just kill them and go to sleep?" I hoped there were just a few.

Kevin shook his head. "I don't think so. There's a lot in there."

I put my flip-flops on, not willing to just go to sleep knowing the bathroom was infested with cockroaches. I reminded myself of the times I'd had to kill spiders and cockroaches in Mexico and braced myself.

We opened the door, and Kevin turned the light on. I jumped back when I saw a sea of black scatter. I was tired and just wanted to go to bed. So I started squashing them with tissue underneath my flip-flops. Kevin came in and helped me decimate as many as we could.

We would turn the light off and on again because they would hide in the light. By the time we didn't see any more, we had finished off about fifty roaches. We decided to check the bedroom to make sure they hadn't gotten in the rest of the room. Sure enough, we found a few more—one big kahuna was even on the headboard.

Earlier that night, Kevin had suggested we sleep in the nude for fun. But after our cockroach adventure, I told him I couldn't bring myself to do it. He concurred.

The next day, we were going snorkeling, which was something neither of us had experienced before. It was a couple hours long excursion because we took a boat tour that brought us to a prime location for spotting underwater life. But the boat ride on the rolling waves made Kevin sick to his stomach.

He thought he was getting better as we snorkeled. The brightly colored fish were a great distraction. But after less than an hour, he told me he had to go back to the boat. As he sat on the rocking boat, his face went white. I gave him a Sprite, hoping that would settle his stomach. Unfortunately, it didn't help.

He started to get up just as his lunch decided to evacuate. A lady who had been sitting on his other side grabbed her purse and fled just in time to avoid the spray.

The boat captain tried to make Kevin feel better, insisting that he wasn't the first and wouldn't be the last to lose his lunch on board.

Kevin still didn't feel the best, since the waves kept pounding. So he laid his head on my shoulder for the ride back to shore. All the while, I pulled my head as far to the other direction as I could politely do to avoid gagging at the smell of vomit still in his mouth.

We now look back at these stories and laugh. Actually, we were laughing just after these events happened, chuckling that we would have some fun stories to tell when we returned.

We had another unexpected side effect of getting married. Along with honeymoon jitters, I developed constipation and even a yeast infection. So we had a late-night excursion, wandering about town until we found a drugstore with itch creams. It was embarrassing at the time, but again, I can laugh about it now.

Even though our honeymoon had its hiccups, it was wonderful. I hate to even call those "hiccups" disappointments because those things that happened were just part of our story. And no story is perfect because when two people give of themselves for each other, their story is beautiful.

My husband and I started something on our honeymoon that has continued to this day. Every night before we go to bed, we will read a chapter of the Bible together. Sometimes it's more than a chapter, and then we will ask what the other needs prayer for, and we'll spend time praying aloud for each other's needs. And then that expanded to praying also for our family and friends, our nieces and nephews, and our future children and their future spouses. I can't even begin to explain what a joy it is to pray with and for each other. It doesn't matter how our day went; once we start having devotions together, earlier frustrations melt away. And your spouse is so incredibly attractive when he is discussing the Word of God and praying for you.

## My Waiting Takeaway

I think it is so important to not only have daily devotions alone with the Lord but also with your spouse, because as you both grow closer to the Lord, you inevitably grow closer together.

I think it's important to find out early on in dating how important God's Word is to a prospective mate. How important is having a relationship with God to them? Are you both on the same page? These are monumentally important questions to ask before marrying someone.

If you've already started dating someone but haven't asked, it's not too late. And ask if he would be willing to pray together now.

Because if he doesn't want to take the time to pray with you while you're dating, chances are he won't want to after you marry him, either.

I can't tell you how much I appreciate having a praying husband. Whenever I get frustrated or stressed about something and I don't know what to do, Kevin will say (after he's let me vent), "Let's pray about this right now." And he will take my hand and lead me in a prayer that always gives me peace and reassurance. Sometimes I get the answer I am looking for right as we pray together.

God cares so much about every part of our lives. He will give us the answers we are looking for if we only ask Him. He wants a relationship with us. He wants us to tell Him everything that is going on in our lives. We just have to remember to sit back and listen to His promptings when He has something to impart to us.

**Your Waiting Step**

Analyze what you think true love is. So many say that there's no such thing as *true love*. I disagree. True love was Christ coming humbly to earth to die and rise for the sins of the entire world. He is the example we have to follow to learn what true love looks like.

True love isn't something you "feel" or don't feel. True love is when Christ in us prompts our behavior to treat others with love. True love is when we sacrifice for someone else. And they in turn will feel that love and sacrifice for us in turn.

True love is choosing every single day that you will stay with this man you have made a commitment to. That is why I don't take the concept of marriage lightly. Unless you can't work through issues and have a Biblical reason to leave, I believe marriage is a covenant for life.

If you go into marriage considering it a life covenant, then you will give it your whole self. You give your spouse your raw, real, open, vulnerable, wholehearted love. And he will then give his whole self in return. It's a beautiful cycle of giving and receiving love.

I carry a reminder in my purse with me of my true love. Instead of carrying around a boarding pass from someone who didn't understand what true love was, I now carry around a photograph—a dashing picture of my husband back in high school.

The photo reminds me of the handsome, innocent boy-turned-man that I married. It reminds me to be grateful and to thank God for fulfilling His promises. And it reminds me of the promise that I made to love, respect, cherish, and adore the most amazing gift God has ever given to me. If you can't tell by now, he was definitely worth waiting for!

### Your Waiting Journal Tips

Think about any expectations of perfection you've held. What misconceptions about true love have you believed? Now replace them with the assurances of Christ's love you've seen in your life. And consider examples of His love found in Scripture, and take some time to thank Him for His abundant love.

### Verse and Prayer

"These things I have spoken to you, that in Me you may have peace. In the world you will have tribulation; but be of good cheer, I have overcome the world." (John 16:33 NKJV)

*Dear heavenly Father,* thank You for Your incomparable love. I pray that You will reveal more of that love to me and help me fully surrender my heart, my plans, and my life to You. And I pray for the peace that passes all understanding to guard my heart against the plans of the enemy. I trust You,

Lord. And I ask that Your peace and love will protect my heart through every season of life. In Jesus's name. Amen.

# A PRAYER FOR YOUR WAITING

Thank you for reading through my journey and love stories. I wanted to leave you with a prayer that I have and will continue to pray for you. . .

*Lord God,* I want to pray for Your precious daughter who has just finished this book. I ask that You cover her with Your embrace of peace and blanket of protection as she journeys through life. I pray that any time she feels brokenhearted, scared, or alone, You will comfort her in the way that only You can—with a love so divine that nothing else can compare.

I ask that You protect her body, mind, and spirit. Hide her from physical danger. Shield her from emotional pain. Hold her heart. I ask that You show her how she can guard her heart. Teach her what it means to wait on You. And I pray that You will inundate her with wisdom straight from heaven. Thank You for giving her discernment in the

Holy Spirit that she will be able to discern where You are leading her.

I pray that You will prepare her heart—whether it's preparation for singleness or for a husband. And I pray that You will prepare the hearts of men to be the husbands You have called them to be. Grow their maturity and their desire to know You more. Allow them to be the strong, tender, caring, loyal leaders You desire them to be.

And I pray that in Your daughter's waiting, she will find perfect peace as she sets her mind and trust in You (Isa. 26:3). I pray that her waiting will be a time of growing, of learning, of trusting, of excitement and enjoyment, and most importantly, a time when she surrenders her heart more and more into Your loving hands. In Jesus's name. Amen.

# ORDER INFORMATION

REDEMPTION
PRESS

To order additional copies of this book, please visit
www.redemption-press.com.
Also available on Amazon.com and BarnesandNoble.com
or by calling toll-free 1-844-2REDEEM.